LETTER OPENERS

Also by Hal Ward

Can Openers: Essays About Life and Love

LETTER OPENERS

OPENERS

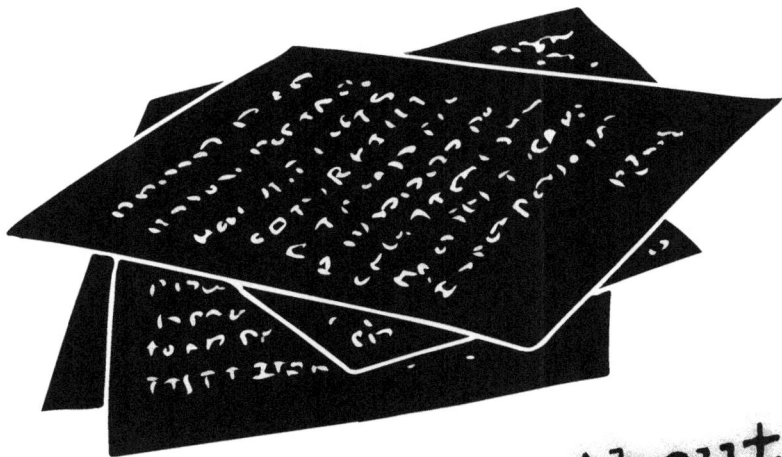

More Essays About Life and Love

HAL WARD

Publishing consultant: David Wogahn
AuthorImprints.com

CONTENTS

LETTER OPENERS

In 2017, I published my first book, entitled *Can Openers*. At the end of the book, I said I was going to take a short break, and return with another book. This is that book. The title *Can Openers* was taken from an essay of the same name. As I finish this book, I realize that I need a title. The title is *Letter Openers*.

The term *letter openers* has at least three meanings. The first meaning is the object, (that looks like a knife), and some people use them to open letters. The second meaning is the beginning of a letter—for example, "Dear Aunt Sophie." The third meaning is that of the recipient, the person who actually receives the letter. That person opens letters. My letters.

This book is meant to be a book of letters to you. These are my letters to you, and you are the letter openers I think about when I use the title. I send letters to many of you, and I know that you open them.

• • •

I started writing letters almost thirty years ago. I remember watching the 1990 Ken Burns documentary *The Civil War*. In one episode, there was a story about a soldier (Sullivan Ballou) who wrote a letter to his wife Sarah just before he left for the Battle of Bull Run. He began the letter, "My Very Dear Wife." By the time his letter arrived, he was dead.

The next day, I wrote a letter to Theresa, and I started it with "My Dearest Theresa." I still start some of my letters to her that way. Maybe my third book will have that title.

• • •

I write a lot of letters. Everyone in my family has a box full of them. I write to my family on every special occasion and after every vacation that we take. I write an end-of-summer letter before my daughters go back to school, and an end-of-year letter that I put in their Christmas stockings. I write these letters because I love to write. I write these letters because it is a way to remind me of important events and memories.

I also write because I hope that someone will read my letters in one hundred years, the same way I read the Civil War letter from Sullivan Ballou to his wife Sarah. I hope that someone remembers me long after I leave this place.

I remember you. I want you to remember me.

• • •

THINKING OUT LOUD, PART I

I knew a man who used the expression "thinking out loud" to describe the process he used to understand the world. He saw things, then he spoke about them, then he understood.

Writing does that for me. I see things, I write about them, and then (sometimes) I understand.

I hope that these essays help you to understand.

★ ★ ★ ★ ★
Why I Write

(I wrote this essay when I started my first blog, called HalWardBlog.com. I was trying to explain why I write. Given that most people don't write anymore, I thought it was worthwhile explaining the "why" behind my blog ...)

I have a friend who likes to say, "I can't wait to hear what I have to say today." What he means is that he learns things about himself when he speaks. He speaks to express himself.

That is why I write. I learn about myself, and about the world, when I write. I sit at the keyboard sometimes, and let the words come out. Sometimes I read what I've written and I think, "I didn't know that ..."

• • •

I have friends who are musicians and artists. Sometimes I watch them play. One of them takes a weekend every year and goes to the Philadelphia Folk Festival. He stays up all night every night and he plays music with his friends. He immerses himself in the music, and time disappears.

He stays up all night playing music in order to express himself. He creates meaning with music, the way I try to create meaning with words.

• • •

Another reason that I write is to digest thoughts. That is a concept I borrowed from a book, by the way.

In the 1961 book *Stranger in a Strange Land*, Robert Heinlein coined the term "grok." I remember reading the book as part of a reading assignment and trying to understand what "grok" meant. It meant "digesting" a thought— more than just observing something. It implied a deeper understanding of things. I think what Robert Heinlein was trying to describe was a process of digesting an experience, and being changed by it.

That is why I write. Sometimes I see something, and I know that it is important when I see it, but I don't immediately understand the importance of it. It takes me some time to digest it and create meaning out of it. Writing is a way for me to create meaning and to express meaning. Sometimes I see something, and I make a note that I should write about it later on. I don't paint, and I don't play music (yet), but I do write. And writing is a way for me to make sense out of what I see in the world.

• • •

Abraham Maslow was a psychologist who proposed a "hierarchy of needs." He suggested that we have some basic needs that must be met (physiological, safety and security, belonging, etc.). Once those most basic needs are met, we are free to focus on "higher needs." The higher needs are things like meaning and purpose, and creativity.

Some people have to focus all of their energy on the most basic needs, like safety, security, and food. I know I am blessed to be able to spend some of my energy on higher needs.

Like writing.

• • •

I have shared with some of you that I am writing a book, one essay at a time. I am writing it for several reasons.

None of those reasons are about money. People don't make much money writing books anymore. There is the occasional runaway bestseller. But most books don't make any money at all. With the advent of electronic books, authors are now paid pennies per book.

I am writing for fun, and for free. Someday I will take this to a printer and make a few copies for friends and family. But unless Oprah comes along and wants to sell my book, I have better things to do with my time than bother trying to make money with this.

★ ★ ★ ★ ★
Who's Your Tribe?

There is a fellow I know who asks people, "Who's your team?" What he means is "What projects are you working on, and which one is most important right now?" I work in an environment where people work on several projects at the same time.

"Who's your team?" means that I need to identify the most important priority at that moment. In an environment with multiple priorities and multiple timelines, "Who's your team?" is a way to identify the number-one priority.

• • •

After a day at work, I come home to a different set of teams. I am a father, a husband, a son, a brother, a cousin, an in-law, and a nephew. I am also a member of several organizations and communities. I am on several teams.

I call them tribes.

Who's my tribe? Which one is most important? What is the best use of my time? Should I go on a date with my wife, attend a board of directors meeting for an organization I serve, or call my father? Should I speak with my daughter, my neighbor, my mother-in-law, or all three? What groups do I belong to? Which ones are most important to me? How should I use my time?

Who's my tribe?

• • •

A few years ago, I started a dialogue with a friend about the meaning of life.. It started off as a joke. I had seen Monty Python's *The Meaning of Life*. (Spoiler alert: this movie is not the place to discover the meaning of life.)

My dialogue about the meaning of life evolved over time into a serious discussion, and now this friend and I speak about it often. I have learned that the meaning of my life is to be the best husband, the best father, the best employee/colleague, and the best member of my tribes that I can be.

• • •

I ask some of my friends the following question: "What is the most important thing in your life?" I have asked many people that question. I've heard answers like *my wife, my husband, my children, my family, my dog, my cat, my investment portfolio, my church, my boat*.

All of those answers are correct. For the people who identified each of those things as the most important thing in their lives, those things are indeed the most important things in their lives. Everyone gets to answer this question for themselves.

I sometimes ask these friends what they spend the most time doing, and whether what they spend time doing is consistent with the most important thing in their lives. If I have a friend who wants to be a classical musician, and he isn't practicing the violin every day, he is not going to become a classical musician.

As you can imagine, I annoy my friends sometimes.

• • •

I have this profound sense that my time is limited, and really important. I have to make choices with my time, and that makes it really precious to me. I once read something that said, "What I do with my day today is really important, because I am giving up a day of my life to do it."

Because of that, I have carved some things out of my life that seem like a waste of my time. I don't watch any TV. I never watched much of it, but I don't watch any now. I read someplace that the average American watches 35 hours of TV a week. Since I don't watch any, the rest of you have to watch more to make up for me.

In place of TV, I spend a lot of time with my family and my tribes. This weekend I am going to have a date with my wife. I am going to have coffee with my older daughter and go driving with my younger daughter. I'm going to take my dog for a long walk in the park.

• • •

What is the most important thing in your life?
   Who's your tribe?

* * * * *
Unintended Consequences

After the terrorist attacks of 9/11, cockpit doors were strengthened and locked. The intention was to keep the bad guys out of the cockpit.

Then a Germanwings pilot intentionally crashed his plane into a mountainside in France.

Who knew that one of the bad guys was going to be flying the plane?

Unintended consequences.

• • •

Fifty years ago, NFL players played football without helmets, or with flimsy leather headgear. Over the years, helmet technology has improved, and now football players play with helmets that are designed to thoroughly protect the head. Yet there have never been so many head injuries in football. Why is that?

One of the unintended consequences of putting on helmets is that players now lead with their heads. On every play, offensive and defensive linemen smash each other in the heads. If you add up the number of head collisions that players experience in pee-wee football, high school football, college football, and then professional football, it's possible that some players experience 10,000 head collisions in their career.

Football has a concussion problem. It looks like a situation of unintended consequences.

• • •

If you take any medication, read the package insert. Go past the pharmacology section and the indications, and you'll find a section entitled "Adverse Reactions." You think of them as side effects.

They are unintended consequences.

With few exceptions, no one ever takes a medication with the intent of experiencing a side effect. But side effects occur often. Check out the percentages of adverse reactions in a package insert.

• • •

Unintended consequences happen in other areas too. Like in our personal lives. It is such a common theme, it is baked into our language. "I didn't sign up for this." It means that we have unintended consequences in our relationships and from our behavior.

I have a running conversation with several people around the theme of "I didn't sign up for this." What we mean, and what our conversations are about, are those unintended consequences of relationships—death, despair, sometimes divorce.

I wonder how often Theresa looks at me and thinks, "I didn't sign up for this"?

• • •

Have you ever seen a TV commercial where two young people enter an elevator, experience an immediate attraction to each other, and then they have a "flash forward" experience where they see the next fifty years of their lives together?

They leave the elevator quickly, without speaking to each other again.

• • •

Another saying in our language is, "Be careful what you wish for, because you just might get it." That's another aspect of unintended consequences. I want something, and at the same time, I don't realize that it isn't good for me.

• • •

I spend a lot of time thinking about predictions. My work involves making predictions. So does my life. Yours life does too.

Where will you work? How much money do you need for retirement? How long will you live? Where will you live? What will your future look like?

There is a good book about making predictions, called *The Signal and the Noise*, by Nate Silver. It is about making predictions in areas like financial markets, mortgage markets, weather, baseball, and earthquakes.

One of the things he says is that it helps to have a lot of historic data if you're making predictions. He notes that it is easier to predict baseball outcomes because there are thousands of records of baseball games, and lots of statistics. It isn't so easy to predict earthquakes, because there aren't that many of them.

How do I predict human relationships, when I haven't had many of them?

• • •

By the way, not all unintended consequences are bad. I asked a lovely young lady for her phone number at a party in 1985. I had no intention of marrying her. I just wanted her phone number.

But I'm glad I asked her. It's working out well so far.

★ ★ ★ ★ ★
This I Believe

In the 1950s, there was a radio show called *This I Believe*. People wrote essays about things that they believed, and then had a few minutes to read those essays on the radio. The show was very popular, and it later became a series of best-selling books of the same name.

I recently attended an online seminar on book writing and book promotion. One of the homework assignments was to write a manifesto. The seminar leader explained that our manifesto should describe what our world view is. In other words, what do we believe in?

In that spirit, I'll add the following saying: A man who stands for nothing will fall for anything.

This is what I believe.

• • •

I believe in altruism. I believe in the value of doing something for other people, without expecting or wanting anything in return.

I donate time and money whenever I can. I mostly try to do so in my local community, so that I know that it will help people close to me, even if I don't know who the recipients are. I like to say, "you might be surprised who gets helped the most." It might be me.

I donate blood. This is a great way to help others and expect nothing in return. My hope is that my eight gallons (and counting) have helped dozens of people who need my blood more than I need it. I will never know who was helped, and that's okay.

I have a little booklet of sayings and quotes. One of the sayings is "As I give to the world, so shall the world give to me." Call that karma if you want. I believe in it. And my life works a lot better when I practice it.

• • •

I believe there is enough to share. I have been blessed in my life with too many things to list here. I live in an affluent area, and my wife and my daughters and I have great gigs to go to every day. We live in a time and a place where we live like princes and princesses. We want for nothing important.

I believe that everyone deserves to have the same opportunity. Everyone. Not just the people with the same beliefs as me or who are of the same political persuasion, or those who root for the same football team. Everyone—no exceptions.

Why limit opportunity for others? Where is the win in that strategy?

• • •

I believe in the value of great public education. The next generation of leaders, teachers, physicians, CEOs, and public servants are sitting in classrooms right now. Why wouldn't we want them to be their very best?

When my wife and I started the process of house hunting in the early 1990s, our real estate agent (who was on the school board of a district nearby) suggested that we go house hunting in the district with the very best schools in the state. We objected at first. We explained that "we will never have children" (not a very accurate prediction, by the way). He explained to us that even if we never had children, the value of our home would always stay strong, because the value of good schools drives the value of home prices. He was right. Even during the mortgage meltdown ten years ago, the value of our house dipped a little bit, and only temporarily.

We have two daughters who have benefited from the value of these great schools. One of our daughters is now running for membership on the local board of education. I think she believes in the value of a great public education, too.

• • •

I believe in the value of financial literacy. I was surprised at how many of you enjoyed the financial essays ("Financial Literacy," "The Ant and the Grasshopper") in my first book, *Can Openers: Essays about Life and Love*.

Most workers no longer receive a pension. Because of that, most of us now have to plan for, and save for, our golden years. Never before have so many of us been responsible for our own financial future. Never before have so many of us been so unprepared to deal with that responsibility.

I believe that everyone should know how to balance a checkbook, pay some bills, maintain a simple budget, and understand how to save and invest for the future.

• • •

I believe in the value of all people. That includes people from every background, and all races, sexes, religions, countries ... you name it, you're important. No exceptions. I've written about this before—I believe in what the plaque on the Statue of Liberty says. I'm also aware of more intolerance currently than during any other time in my lifetime. I can change that in my little corner of the world. I believe that.

• • •

I believe that I need your help. I am not a "self-made man." I am where I am because of other people. I am not a lone wolf. I received a great education, and great role models helped me become who I am. I wouldn't be where I am without them.

I think it is important that I try to give back, in some small way, what I so freely received.

I believe in the value of companionship. As I have gotten older, I have learned the value of human interaction, especially with those to whom I am closest. I need human interaction every day. Even though I am an introvert, I am not supposed to be alone. I am better off for having other people in my life. I do a crossword puzzle with my best friend every day. There is a reason for that, and it isn't about the puzzle.

• • •

I believe in the value of hard work, and the importance of discipline. I know a lot of people who can't (or don't) work. I wouldn't trade places with any of them. Even the wealthy ones. I think work is about a lot more than money. Work keeps me mentally and physically active. It helps my self-esteem. I'm grateful for the opportunity to work, and I hope that I'm able to continue working for many more years to come.

I am better off having work in my life. It provides structure and discipline for me in every area of my life, including my social life, diet, exercise, finance, and recreation. I value every part of my life more because I am so busy.

At the same time, I am aware that a lot of people don't have a job to go to every day. There are lots of reasons for this (retirement, disability, unemployment, prison, welfare). Regardless of the cause, none of it looks appealing to me. I want to continue working for as long as I am physically and mentally able to do so.

• • •

I believe that miracles happen in the lives of people. I've seen several of them occur. I've seen people with impossible diseases experience cures. I've seen people who were once hopeless and homeless experience transformations that allow them to be incredibly productive members of society. I've seen people who were once immobilized by illness, who now lead lives with more energy than I have.

Maybe "miracles" sounds too dramatic. But if not a miracle, what other word would you use?

• • •

I believe that I can make a difference with my writing and my storytelling. I believe that my writing is pretty good. I regularly receive feedback from readers about how meaningful my essays have been to them. One friend told me that he read "My Mother's Day Card" three times, and cried every time. Two people this week told me that they wanted to be more like "ants" and less like "grasshoppers." I believe that when I write well, I can connect with people as well as anyone.

I believe in the power of personal stories. Those stories convey meaning in a way that other written forms cannot. Stories are memorable because they involve people that we know. I remember stories, because I remember people in my life.

After the publication of my first book, I held my first book event. I was lucky enough to have it take place at the Plays and Players Theater in Philadelphia. Broad Street Ministry did all of the heavy lifting and arranged an evening that I am grateful for. Fifty of my friends, family, and readers attended. It was a special evening. For several weeks, those who attended mentioned how much they enjoyed it.

What made it really special was that we told stories, and now we have new stories to tell. That night in Philadelphia was my first book event, but it won't be the last. I promise.

My writing moves people. I know that. I think I do it well. What I don't do well (yet) is building an audience. I believe that building an audience doesn't just happen for most authors. It takes work, and I haven't done much of that work yet.

Stay tuned and I'll share with you, sometime soon, what I'm going to do to start increasing the size of my tribe.

This I believe.

★ ★ ★ ★ ★

The Watering Hole

When I was young, I used to watch wildlife shows on TV. I remember watching *Mutual of Omaha's Wild Kingdom* with Marlin Perkins. For a little kid from Northeast Philadelphia, watching wildlife on TV was as close to the real thing as I could get.

Marlin Perkins would narrate each episode, and his younger sidekick, Jim, would interact with the wild animals. I thought that was funny.

Marlin was probably sipping iced tea under a shady tree while Jim was wrestling with a lion.

• • •

The old wildlife shows often took place at watering holes. Watering holes are oases, or places where there is water and food. They are miraculous places, really. In the middle of some of the most desolate locations on earth, there are these small areas of water and food, and ultimately, of life.

All of the animals come to the watering hole. Big and small, predators and prey, it doesn't matter. Every animal needs water to survive. Most of the wildlife shows would show interactions between different kinds of animals. For example, some small birds might be eating parasites off the back of a rhinoceros. They called that "symbiosis"—a "win-win" relationship. The rhinoceros wins, because it gets rid of the parasites on its back. The birds win, because they get to eat.

(My copy editor sent me a note about this. She reported that "it turns out that they also drink the rhino's blood, making sores take longer to heal. So not a complete win-win.")

(I must be the only author who has a copy editor who fact-checks me on parasitic biology.)

• • •

I have oases like this in my life; places where I go and hang out with the other wild animals. Places like coffee shops, and diners, and houses of worship. My friends and family and I come to these places for more than water. We come to these places for ideas, and for knowledge.

One of my favorite oases is the dinner table. At my dinner table, we have great conversations. We exchange ideas and share thoughts. As a result, we grow, and our minds change. I try to surround myself with people who know more than I do, and who are willing to teach me.

I'm not done learning yet. That's why I go to the watering hole.

* * * * *

The Drug Overdose Epidemic

(This was originally published June 8, 2017 at halwardblog.com.)

A month ago, my father texted me and asked, "What is an opioid?" I don't usually pick up the phone when he texts me, but this time I did. He said that he was watching a documentary on the opioid epidemic, and the documentary never defined what an opioid is.

You probably know this, but just in case: "opioid" and "opiate" are used interchangeably, and describe a class of drugs that were originally derived from opium, which is extracted from the poppy plant. Examples of drugs in this class include opium, morphine, codeine, heroin, fentanyl, carfentanil, hydrocodone and oxycodone.

Opioids are very potent pain relievers. Unfortunately, they are highly addictive, because for some people they can also be enormously pleasurable when first taken.

• • •

The *New York Times* published an article this week on drug overdose deaths. Check it out at this link:

https://www.nytimes.com/interactive/2017/06/05/upshot/opioid-epidemic-drug-overdose-deaths-are-rising-faster-than-ever.html?_r=0

In the article, the *New York Times* estimates that approximately 59,000 Americans died of overdose deaths in 2016. In one chart, it compares that rate to the peak fatality rates for car accidents, shootings, and deaths from HIV. All of those rates are lower than the current rate of overdose deaths referenced in the article.

If an airliner with 160 people crashed today, killing everyone on board, within an hour every network would have special programming about it.

You would know the name of the airline, the flight number, and details about all of the passengers.

An airliner full of Americans dies every day from drug overdoses, and no network is breaking into their regular programming about it.

• • •

I've done a great deal of reading about this, and here's what I've gleaned, as of June 2017. There are many reasons for the increase in overdose deaths in America. One is that prescription pain medication has become much more potent, and much more available. Several years ago, a new oral agent (oxycodone, marketed as Oxycontin), was approved for marketing. This drug has become widely available not only for prescription use, but also for abuse.

At the same time, the supply of heroin has increased and the cost has decreased. Heroin is now much more available, much more widely used, and less expensive than when I was growing up. Supposedly, the cost of a dose of heroin is now less than the cost of a bottle of beer. When I was in high school, the "gateway drugs" were marijuana and alcohol. Not now.

One other reason is that other very potent drugs (fentanyl and carfentanil) are being sold as heroin. Fentanyl is more potent than heroin, and carfentanil is said to be 1000-5000 times more potent than heroin.

If someone thinks that they are injecting heroin but receives either fentanyl or carfentanil, they are going to die.

• • •

The opioid epidemic is not some far-away problem that only happens in a newspaper. It is a local problem that is killing people who live near me. At the time of this writing, drug overdoses now look like this in my area:

Last week, two men died of heroin overdoses not too far from where I live. What made their overdoses even more remarkable was that they were house managers in a local halfway house. They were the ones in charge of oversight at their facility.

The same week, eight addicts died of overdoses in another small town not too far from where I live.

A recent local high school graduate died of an opiate overdose a few weeks ago.

A *Philadelphia Inquirer* article (https://www.inquirer.com/philly/health/addiction/Fatal-overdoses-in-Phila-surged-in-2016-task-force-launched.html)noted that Philadelphia had 900 fatal overdoses in 2016. Bucks County had 185. The same article included an old estimate of 10 fatal overdoses a day in Pennsylvania—and then noted that that estimate might be low now.

Ten people lose their lives every day in my state from a preventable problem. And either we have become used to it, or we don't know about it.

• • •

This is a complicated problem with no easy answers. It would be intellectually lazy to say, "just cut off the supply." The supply is not just illegal drugs like heroin. It also includes prescription drugs that are diverted. The problem is not just at our borders; it is also in our doctors' offices and our pharmacies and our own medicine cabinets.

I read that the United States consumes 80% of the world supply of opiates. We have 4% of the world population. There is something wrong with that.

• • •

Fortunately there is hope. Treatment exists. I know two young men who recently were in treatment for opioid addiction, and both are now in recovery.

But every day that they remain in recovery, an average of 160 Americans are going to die from drug overdoses.

And I don't know what to do about that.

* * * * *

The Comments Section

Have you ever taken the time to read an article online, and then read the comments section? Have you ever been bothered with the nature of online comments?

The *Guardian* newspaper in England published an article about their study of the comments attached to their online articles. At the time the study was published, there had been 70 million comments attached to articles in the *Guardian*. About 1.4 million comments (2%) had to be blocked because they were inappropriate.

The *Guardian* analyzed the inappropriate comments and the articles they were attached to. The newspaper learned that the majority of the authors who received the most hateful comments were women and minorities.

The *Guardian* situation isn't unique. The same thing happens on a number of websites and technologies. I have read posts from people who have stopped using Facebook and Twitter because they couldn't stand the hateful feedback they received.

• • •

I used to allow comments on my blog. When I started, I noted that I would allow comments as long as they were respectful. But I eventually had to turn the comments off.

Those of you who know me know how to reach me. I appreciate your feedback, and the guidance you've provided me as I continue to build my website.

• • •

I recently wrote a post called "The Bill of Responsibilities." I was thinking about online comments when I wrote that blog. My point was that we are more concerned with our rights than our responsibilities.

One example is the freedom of speech. That is a freedom guaranteed by the Constitution. However, it carries some limits and some responsibilities. The classic one is that no one should yell "fire" in a crowded movie theater (unless there is a fire, of course), because people could be harmed in the resulting panic.

Hate speech is not protected by the First Amendment. Google the phrase "arrests for hate speech" and look how many results there are (at the time of this writing there were 525,000). People who spew hate speech are starting to be prosecuted as criminals.

I hope that helps. I appreciate the place that online technology has in our lives. My hope is that a few haters don't ruin the technology for everyone else.

★ ★ ★ ★ ★
Spider Webs

I go to a park near our home at least once a week. I take my dog there (or maybe he takes me there, I'm not sure). We take a walking trail that is about one mile long. There is an icehouse on the trail. Icehouses were structures built before the invention of refrigerators. They stored ice underground, where it was cooler than it was above ground.

I pass this icehouse at least fifty times a year, and I hadn't even glanced at it for years, until recently. I walked up to it and examined it. I even tried to open the door, but it was locked.

• • •

Not too long ago I was walking to the mailbox, and I noticed a mound next to our driveway. It was a cool morning, and everything was covered with dew. Because the mound was wet with dew, I noticed that it was also covered with spider webs. I usually ignore this mound. I'm so focused on getting somewhere that I don't take the time to look at it.

• • •

I have a friend who I see every week. When I first met him twenty-five years ago, he was about the same age that I am now. He was robust, mobile, and very active. Now he needs a wheelchair, is losing his vision, and cannot drive. He and I know some other fellows in our community who need walkers, canes, and crutches to get around.

I take it for granted that I am always going to be mobile and active, but my friend is an example to me that that is not true. My active times are not permanent, and they are not guaranteed.

• • •

We just completed a minor remodeling of our home. We had a couple of bedrooms that were underused. We used them as "junk drawers." We emptied them out, had them gutted, and converted them into a guest bedroom and an office.

The guest bedroom was built with the idea that we may need to have people living with us sometime. We don't have anyone in mind, but there are three houses on our street where there are three generations living under one roof. That is becoming more common in our society, and my family thought that we should be prepared for that possibility.

• • •

I take my life and my health for granted most of the time. I take all of you being in my life for granted. I'm not proud of that. But it's true. Then once in a while, something happens, and I see how things really are. Change happens and I notice it.

Sometimes it takes a change in temperature for me to notice the spider webs.

* * * * *

RSVP

There have been articles published recently in the *New York Times* and on HuffPost on the topic of "ghosting." Ghosting is when someone stops responding to you and pretends that you don't exist. They are pretending that you are invisible and that they can't see you. The articles describe how it happens in dating. Basically, if you're dating someone, and they stop responding to all communication from you, they are ghosting you.

Ghosting is happening in other places too.

I know someone who recently went through three rounds of interviews with a Fortune 500 company. They promised her a response by a certain date. Now they are not responding to her calls or emails.

I was scheduled to fly the friendly skies last week. My airline canceled my flight less than twenty-four hours before takeoff. I had to drive twelve hours each way, because they could not place me on a flight in time. I sent a note to their customer service department and asked for some compensation. I'm still waiting for a response. I'm not holding my breath.

We host parties at Chez Ward, or a restaurant, once a century or so. When we do, we ask for replies in the form of an RSVP. "RSVP" stands for "répondez s'il vous plaît," meaning "please respond." We know that people are busy, so we ask for emails, or texts, or calls; whatever is easiest. And yet, many people don't respond.

I know that I will sound like a crotchety old fart when I say this, but when did it become okay for us to stop responding to each other? I realize that saying no to someone isn't easy, but we all deserve a human response to a human question. I understand that sometimes the answer is no. I'd like to hear it, rather than trying to interpret silence.

* * * * *
Retiring

In the past month, two people have asked me when I'm retiring. But neither one called it "retiring." They called it "transitioning." I'm assuming they meant "retiring," and not "dying."

• • •

I know three people who retired in their forties. They were successful business owners who sold their businesses. They played a lot of golf, and they did some traveling. Two of the three people went back to work within a year of retiring. I guess they got tired of playing golf.

I also have an uncle who is in his late eighties and works every day. He doesn't do it for the money. He works every day because he loves what he does.

• • •

If I were given the choice between stopping work in my forties or loving my work in my eighties, I would rather love my work in my eighties.

Right now I love what I do for a living. I'm lucky that I have stimulating work, and I work with really good people. I love having someplace to go every day, where there are interesting problems to solve, and really smart people who know how to solve them. What I really want is to love what I do, and have the ability to continue to do it.

A positive side benefit of working is that I value my free time more. My experience has been that if I have too much free time (like on a long vacation), I just fritter it away. But when I only have a little bit of free time, I make the most of it.

• • •

I realize that I may not be able to work into my eighties. I don't know anyone in my industry who is still working at that age. I might have to find other things to do with my time. What would I do with my time?

My wife and I started doing charitable work a few years ago. We have been volunteering with a few organizations, and we serve on the boards for two of them. I'd like to increase that type of work, if I have the time to do so in the future. I am reminded of a saying that goes something like, "Of whom much is given, much is expected." I have been given a lot in my life, and I hope to repay the favor.

My wife and children love to travel, so I'd like to help make that possible for them, and join them. (You noticed that I didn't say "I love to travel." I've traveled overseas almost 100 times now. I don't love airplanes and hotels anymore. I don't love "getting there." But I still love exploring, once I "get there.")

• • •

I think that the word "retiring" means "quitting" for a lot of people. For a lot of people, retiring is the end of something. I'm not ready for the end of anything yet.

★ ★ ★ ★ ★
Radical Hospitality

My wife and I started volunteering at Broad Street Ministry (BSM) a few years ago. The first time I volunteered, I saw a big green sign on the wall that said "Radical Hospitality Practiced Here." What is "Radical Hospitality"? This is what I have learned.

When I first volunteered at BSM, I assumed that they were focused on serving meals to the homeless. While that is part of what they do, I heard a staff member say, "It's not about what you think it's about." What he meant is that the meals that are offered at BSM are a way of welcoming vulnerable people through the doors. Once they are there, they learn that BSM offers a variety of vitally important social services to this community.

The list of social services can be found at http://www.broadstreethospitality.org/social-services/, and includes personal care items, a clothing closet, and therapeutic arts. Partner services include case management, medical services, psychiatric and behavioral services, dental services, HIV testing and counseling, and benefits counseling.

• • •

One of the most interesting services (to me) is the BSM mail service. Pretend for a minute that you are homeless. Pretend that you are about to complete a job application, a benefits application, or an application to request a service. After you enter your name on the form, what is ALWAYS the next piece of information that is requested? Your address, of course. You cannot complete any type of form in our society without providing a mailing address. What do you use as your address if you are homeless?

BSM provides a mailing address and mail service to over 3,000 people in their area. That is a remarkable feat. It means that not only do they provide a mailing address, but they also provide the support to receive and distribute mail to all 3,000 of those people.

That is radical hospitality.

• • •

The first time I served a meal at Broad Street Ministry, I was touched by the contrast with other places where I have served or distributed meals. When I walked into the dining area, there was music playing (Frank Sinatra, on my first day). There were decorations at every table. Each table was arranged "in the round," so that guests had the opportunity to socialize.

Note that I just used the word "guests." Broad Street Ministry taught me that. The people who come to dine at BSM are guests. At BSM, every guest is welcomed with open arms. They are encouraged to dine, to celebrate and socialize with friends, to take advantage of the available social services, and to break bread in a beautiful setting.

Do you know what radical hospitality looks like? How about having an executive chef, a sous chef, and two cooks to prepare meals for the guests at Broad Street Ministry? The food that they prepare is delicious, nutritious, and expertly plated. It is as good as any restaurant that I frequent in my community. I mean that. I am honored to serve the dishes that they create, every time that I have the opportunity to do so.

• • •

There is an inscription on the Statue of Liberty that describes radical hospitality. Written by Emma Lazarus, it reads in part,

Give me your tired, your poor,
Your huddled masses yearning to breathe free,
The wretched refuse of your teeming shore.
Send these, the homeless, tempest-tost to me.
I lift my lamp besides the golden door!

Radical hospitality means lifting our lamp to the homeless and vulnerable residents of Philadelphia, and welcoming them. That is what Broad Street Ministry does every day. They open their doors to the homeless and vulnerable community and make them feel welcome.

Every time I volunteer at BSM, I am awakened spiritually, and I feel better about the world for several days. I tell my friends, "You might be surprised who is helped the most." It might be me.

★ ★ ★ ★ ★
Politics as Unusual

My family attended a graduation party recently. We have been friends with the hosts for twenty years. The party was wonderful—good friends, good food, good fun. The hosts are local businesspeople. They are the kind of people that you want as next-door neighbors. They coached Little League games, and they volunteer in the community. They are what I call "good people."

The only problem is that their political beliefs are much different than mine.

• • •

Nancy Reagan died in March of 2016. After the funeral, a photo was taken of George W. Bush and Hillary Clinton at a reception. They were embracing each other, and smiling. You don't see Republicans and Democrats doing that much anymore.

In January 2005, in response to the devastating tsunami in the Pacific Ocean, former President George H.W. Bush and former President Clinton worked together, at the request of President Obama, to raise money to aid tsunami victims. The work was not Republican work, or Democratic work. It was life-saving work. And the two former presidents worked together to help save lives and rebuild nations.

• • •

I have a lot of friends who sit on the other side of the political aisle from me. I know their beliefs because I speak to them, and I follow their Facebook feeds.

These are good and decent people who do life-saving and life-changing work. When I say that they do "life-saving and life-changing work," I mean that.

Can they really all be wrong, just because they disagree with me?

• • •

When I was younger, I recall politicians working in a bipartisan manner. Politicians on both sides of the political spectrum worked together to get work done. It doesn't seem like that happens much anymore. It seems to me that it is more important to make "the other side" wrong than it is to work with "the other side" to accomplish things.

When did we lose the ability to work with people that we don't agree with? Have we completely lost the ability to work with each other? Can we disagree without being disagreeable?

• • •

I reserve the right to work with other people of all backgrounds and all beliefs. I may not agree with all of them about all things. But I want to maintain the ability to meet most of them halfway, so that we can accomplish things together.

I guess that excludes me from political service.

★ ★ ★ ★ ★
Pandora's Box

(This was originally published on July 11, 2016 at halwardblog.com.)

Pandora's box is an idea rooted in Greek mythology. The box was something that was opened (against advice). After the box was opened, there were unintended consequences.

• • •

The automobile was invented by Karl Benz in 1885. I wasn't there, but that's what the internet says, so it must be true. I spend a lot of time in my car, so I think about cars a lot.

I wonder what Karl Benz would think about traffic jams, drunk driving, car accidents, and LA freeways. I wonder what he would have thought about OPEC, and wars fought over access to oil.

When he invented the automobile, I'm sure he wasn't thinking about road rage.

• • •

The Wright brothers' first flight at Kitty Hawk was in 1903. I spend a lot of time on airplanes, so I think about air travel a lot, too. That first flight happened around the same time that my grandparents were born. At the time of my grandparents' birth, no one said, "let's go to the airport," because there was no airport to go to.

I wonder what Orville and Wilbur Wright would say about 9/11. I wonder what their reaction would be to cockpit voice recorders, security lines at O'Hare Airport, or sitting in the middle seat on a red-eye flight.

• • •

Antibiotics did not exist 100 years ago. Penicillin was discovered in the 1920s, and the sulfonamides were discovered in the 1930s. Penicillin was widely used in the 1940s as a result of commercial production.

When Alexander Fleming discovered penicillin in his petri dish in the 1920s, I wonder what his reaction would have been to antibiotic resistance and super-organisms?

• • •

The first corporate pension plan was created by the American Express Company in 1875. My grandparents and parents expected to receive pensions as part of their lifetime employment with one company. Pensions lost popularity in the 1970s, and started being replaced with employee-funded plans, like 401(k)s. The point of employee-funded plans was to shift the responsibility for retirement savings over to us as individuals.

When we turned the responsibility for retirement savings over to us, we opened a Pandora's box. The median (midpoint) 401(k) balance in the United States is less than $30,000. (For fans of statistics, the average 401(k) balance is over $100,000. The average is higher than the midpoint because a small group of people have very large 401(k) balances. But the "midpoint" of balances is about $30,000). That $30,000, plus social security, is all that we have saved for our retirement. That $30,000 balance needs to last a lot longer than it did when my grandparents were saving for retirement. Their expected lifespan was only seventy years. My physician and my financial planner say that I should plan on living to ninety-five.

Our parents and grandparents were raised expecting to be taken care of by their pensions. Now we have no pensions, and many of us have no retirement savings.

· · ·

I am not opposed to progress. I love progress. My life is richer and more rewarding as a result of air travel and automobiles, and I imagine I might not be alive without antibiotics.

My point is that the inventors of planes, cars, antibiotics, and pensions could never have imagined how we would use their inventions.

✶ ✶ ✶ ✶ ✶
Out of Time

A few years ago, Justin Timberlake starred in a move called *In Time*. It was a futuristic movie about a society where the currency was time, not money. Every person had a chip implanted in their arm, with a "bank" of time in the chip. The time in the chip could be exchanged for goods and services.

When the time ran out on the chip, the person with the chip died.

• • •

The movie examined what would happen in a society where time was used as currency. What would people do for an additional day, or week, or month of life? What would you do if you were down to your last twenty-four hours?

In the movie, just like in real life, some people stole other peoples' time. Also in the movie, just like in real life, some people gave their time to others. Except in the movie, giving away some time meant giving away some life.

• • •

I remember watching the movie and being moved by the parallels between time and money. We live in a society where we act like we have all of the time in the world, and act like money is a precious, limited resource.

I suppose money is limited, to some extent. But there is a lot of it out there, and I probably have enough. Not as much as I necessarily want, but probably as much as I need.

I am starting to have an awareness that I don't have as much time as I would like. Here is an example: if I live to the age of 95 (no guarantees about that), I will live about 34,675 days. That would mean that I have about 14,600 days left.

I spent about $14,600 on my last car. I'm kind of frugal, so I was reluctant to part with that $14,600. I spent a lot of time (read that phrase again) thinking about parting with $14,600.

What do I think about parting with my last 14,600 days? Do I treat my time with as much care as I treat my money? I need to remember that if I give away some of my time, I am giving away some of my life.

* * * * *

Out of Gas

On the way to work, I pass a gas station. I pass that same gas station every day on the way home. I get gas at this gas station every two days (I drive 240 miles in those two days).

Except about six weeks ago, the gas station placed orange traffic cones next to the pumps, and put signs marked "Pumps Not Working" over the credit card readers at each pump. The pumps have been out of order for over a month now.

This is not a little gas station. They have twelve gas pumps at this station, and it was often full, with twelve cars pumping gas at the same time. It is located on a busy corner, on a main road in my area.

They have a mini-market at this gas station, but there aren't a lot of cars stopping there anymore. There are lots of other gas stations with mini-markets in our area, so they are losing more business every day.

I don't know why, but this gas station fascinates me, in a morbid way. Every time I pass it, I look over to see if they have resolved the issue with the gas pumps. I have the same reaction with this gas station as I do when I pass a car accident. I can't help looking at the wreckage.

How does a gas station go without gas pumps for six weeks? I've been tempted to walk in and ask, "What is going on here?" but I haven't had the nerve.

What happened?

• • •

It's not just my local gas station that's slowly sinking. Retail stores are closing all around. I've read several articles recently about mall and chain stores closing for good. The list includes brands like RadioShack, Payless ShoeSource, HHGregg, American Apparel, The Limited, and Bebe.

• • •

We went to one of our favorite restaurants a few weeks ago. It is a wonderful little Italian place. We usually get there early to beat the rush. Normally by the time we are done with our meal, the place is full, and there is a line for a table.

But this time, no one came in. We kept waiting for the crowds to come, but no crowds came. I had this uneasy feeling that ours was the only meal that they were going to prepare that night.

What happened?

• • •

There is something really unsettling to me about driving by a gas station without gas, or going into a restaurant without any other diners. It feels like failure and death to me. There are two businesses that are failing in my community, and I don't know why. People still need gas, and people still go out to eat, but they aren't getting gas at this gas station, and they aren't eating at this restaurant.

What happened?

• • •

JUST FOR LAUGHS

Once in a while I write a funny essay. Sometimes it is funny by design, and other times it is funny accidentally. Here are a few of each style.

* * * * *

The Worst Campaign Manager Ever

A few months ago, my daughter decided to run for a seat on our township school board. I was pleased with her decision. She wants to give back to our schools, because our schools have been very good to her. She needed a campaign manager. I was surprised when she selected me.

There is no job description for this role, but if there were, I know that it would include traits like "understands campaign law," "highly organized," and "people person."

Let's start with "understands campaign law." I have no experience in this area, and this is a complicated area! I will give you one example: In order to obtain a position on our local ballot, you must have a petition signed by a certain number of voters who are registered in each party. In order to have someone sign your petition

1) that person must be registered to vote in our region;

2) that person must be registered to vote in the party whose petitions they are signing (in other words, Republicans sign the Republican petition, Democrats sign the Democratic petition);

33

3) they have to sign their name exactly the same way they are registered, or their signature doesn't count;

4) they have to write the name of our township correctly. (Maybe that doesn't sound like a big deal, but it is if you live in Tredyffrin Township.)

The last requirement is where it gets really complicated: a Republican who is registered in the township must hand the petition to Republican signers, and a Democrat must hand the petition to Democratic signers. So if you go to a house with one Democratic voter and one Republican voter, you must have two people to hand the petitions to them. I'm not making this up.

I did not understand any of this when we started. My daughter had to explain it all to me.

Let's move to "highly organized." That's not me. I have to keep a dozen lists just to maintain the appearance of being organized. But I would describe myself as "highly disorganized, masquerading as organized."

Finally, "people person." I like people. Really, I do. But I struggle with the idea of meeting a lot of them all at once. Read my essay "Being an Introvert" for more on this. Luckily I am not the one who has to go door to door, shaking hands.

• • •

So let's agree that I meet none of the requirements for the Campaign Manager Job Description. My candidate (my daughter) is in big trouble . . .

(Postscript—my daughter won her election, even though I was the Worst Campaign Manager Ever.)

★ ★ ★ ★ ★
Dad-Speak

My daughters tell me that I have a language of my own. I did not believe them, so they compiled a list of some of the things that I say. They call these phrases "Dad-speak." I have provided some definitions for my Dad-speak:

Dad-speak	The definition
Ressies	This is short for "restaurant reservation," as in "should I make ressies for Friday night?"
Appies	This is short for "appetizers," as in "should we order a couple of appies?"
Crossie	This is short for "crossword puzzle," as in "would you like to do a crossie with me?"
Nanners	Bananas
Sangweech	This is a sandwich, made with a slice of pizza plus whatever else is in the refrigerator, preferably pasta. Because pizza doesn't have enough carbs all by itself.
Over/under	This is what I ask when I wonder how much of something will occur. For example, "over/under on how many gallons of gas I need to fill my tank," or "over/under on the cost of this repair bill." I set the line, and my family picks over or under.
It's good to have the band back together	What I say at family dinners. I think we should do a reunion tour.
Thanks for coming out to play	What I say to friends and family when we socialize.
BGDD	Big Guy Daddy Dude. How I used to sign letters to my daughters. Up until ... okay, it is still how I sign letters to my daughters.

Dad-speak	The definition
WCME	Worst Campaign Manager Ever. That's me.
Iggles	My favorite football team, the Philadelphia Eagles.
Ac-uh-me	Where we shop for groceries, the Acme.
Inkwire	The location of our crossword puzzles, the *Philadelphia Inquirer.*
Dingleberry duty	This involves cleaning Darwin, our dog. I'm not providing any more details, it's gross.

For my friends and family, maybe we can get the band back together. I'll make ressies, we can start with appies. I will thank you for coming out to play. When I get home I'll do a crossie with my sweetie.

★ ★ ★ ★ ★
Ten Things My Dog Darwin and I Have in Common:

1. We are both grey
2. We both come from the mean streets of Northeast Philadelphia
3. We are both crazy about Theresa, Heather, and Dylan
4. We both snore
5. We both make funny faces if you put peanut butter on the roofs of our mouths
6. We both think we may be done making little Schnoodles
7. Neither one of us is afraid of the neighborhood fox
8. Neither one of us can see without glasses
9. Our eyebrows get crazy if you don't groom us at least once a month
10. Both of us get in trouble when we pee on the next-door neighbor's mailbox

★ ★ ★ ★ ★
Strawberry Island

My family and I have an ongoing dialogue about "foods we can live without." What we mean by this is, "what foods could we do without for the rest of our lives, and not miss them?"

The foods on this list give me no pleasure at all. It would be okay with me if these foods were sent to a desert island, never to be seen again. I call that island "Strawberry Island," because one of the foods I would send there is strawberries. This is my list of Strawberry Island foods:

1. strawberries
2. pickles
3. olives
4. tea
5. balsamic vinaigrette
6. cake
7. apples
8. key lime pie
9. pesto sauce
10. white bread

You may be thinking "you just haven't had the RIGHT olives," or "wait until you try really FRESH strawberries!" I've had olives in Greece, tea in England and Japan, and picked my own strawberries and apples. My daughter brought aged balsamic vinegar from Modena, Italy. I really get no pleasure from any of these foods.

The funny thing is that my family loves some of the foods on this list. They love olives (Theresa sometimes serves a bowl of olives with dinner, and has an apple every day with her lunch). They really enjoy strawberries, and they don't mind that I am not eating cake, because it means more cake for them.

If you bake cupcakes for them, they will be overjoyed. My reaction is "yay."

· · ·

I like a number of foods that other people do not like (and that I did not like when I was young). I like brussels sprouts, beets, pepper, and garlic. When I was younger I did not enjoy any of those.

What foods would you send to Strawberry Island?

★ ★ ★ ★ ★
My Frying-Pan Toilet

(I wrote this essay during a trip to Japan in 2015. Toilets in Japan can be complicated.)

I'm staying at a hotel 7000 miles from home. My hotel room has a toilet (that's good). The toilet has a seat warmer (in theory, not so bad). The seat warmer is set to "cook Hal's derrière" (that's bad). And I can't figure out how to turn off the derrière cooker.

So I decided to check the toilet instructions. See the photo below for the instructions.

"Never immerse the shower toilet or splash it with water." Not a problem for me; I gave up splashing toilets several years ago.

"Never disassemble or remodel the shower toilet." Again, not a problem, because I left my tools at home. If they want to remodel the place themselves, go ahead.

"When the toilet seat is used by ... people who cannot adjust the temperature themselves, turn off the seat heater." This is where I have a problem with the instructions. I am the person using the toilet seat. I cannot adjust the heat. So how am I supposed to turn off the heater?!

"If the toilet seat is used for a long time without turning off the heater, there is a danger of low temperature burns."

It's going to be a long week . . .

* * * * *

My Lonely Facebook Like

A few weeks ago, I posted a photo on Facebook. It was a photo from a bus station in Tokyo. I noted that the bus that I take to the airport leaves from the third floor.

My point was that I have to go upstairs to catch my bus. Buses usually leave from the ground floor. I thought it was sort of weird that a bus departed from the third floor. (It really does leave from the third floor. There are elevated highways here.)

That post received one Facebook like.

I didn't know that it was POSSIBLE to get only one like. In the history of Facebook, no other post ever met such silence. People post puppy photos and get ten million likes.

Not my post. If a post could produce the sound of crickets chirping, this one would have.

I now take a lot of abuse at home about my lonely Facebook like.

* * * * *

Bug Duty

Almost everyone has a phobia. For my family, that phobia is bugs.

Because my family has a bug phobia, I am in charge of Bug Duty. "Bug Duty" means that I need to drop whatever I am doing to kill bugs, whenever they are found in our house. Last night, a moth flew into the bedroom area upstairs. I was woken in the middle of the night (actually about 10:30) in order to perform Bug Duty. Unfortunately, I couldn't get the moth. He escaped me. I am now alone in the house. My family moved out of the house.

That is quite a phobia.

* * * * *

Animal House

It's been a few years since I lived in a dormitory, but I had some wonderful experiences while doing so. Here are some of my favorites:

Toilet Ball: My roommates and I spent hours playing a game that we invented. One of my roommates had a Nerf football. We set the football up on a tee in our kitchen, down the hallway from the bathroom. It was about a thirty-foot distance from the kitchen to the bathroom. The goal was to kick the football off the tee, down the hallway, and into the toilet. This was a difficult task. It sometimes took thirty to forty-five minutes for one of us to kick the football into the toilet. Once one of us did that, the game was over, because the football was a sponge, and took a couple of days to dry out.

Total cost to play: one Nerf football

Fire Extinguisher Wars: My roommates and I were bored one Saturday night (why was Saturday night the night for this sort of thing?). One of us (not me, I promise) started this by opening a fire extinguisher and spraying everyone with foam. Hilarity (and lots of fire extinguishers and lots of foam) ensued.

Total cost to play: several $25 campus fines (which was a lot of money in 1979), plus cleanup costs.

The Roast Beef Fire: I now understand that it is important to avoid any contact with the red-hot cooking element at the top inside part of a toaster oven. I did not understand that in 1979. My roommate and I tried to cook a roast beef inside a toaster oven. The roast beef expanded during cooking, came in contact with the heating element, and caught fire.

Total cost to play: no cost because we put the fire out in time. We saved ourselves the cost of a $25 fine by not using

a fire extinguisher (see "Fire Extinguisher Wars" above).
We also salvaged most (but not all) of the roast beef.

The Great Squirrel Adventure: We lived in a first-floor dormitory. The windows had no screens. One spring afternoon, we left our windows open. A squirrel somehow came into our room through the window. The squirrel was as unhappy about this turn of events as we were. My roommate and I chased the squirrel around the room, trying to get him to leave out the window. Unfortunately, he jumped into a poster on the wall (it must have looked like outside to him). He fell stunned onto one of the beds. My roommate picked him up, and gently took him outside. The squirrel quickly recovered, ran away, and told his family about two fellows who set a roast beef on fire.

Total cost to play: free

The Three-Day Practical Joke: Our next-door neighbors were two fellows who became good friends of ours. They shared something with us about their living arrangement. If either of them brought a young lady back to their room for the evening, the "signal" for this would be that they would put the chain lock on the door. In other words, if one of them came back to their room with this arrangement, and the chain lock was on, they needed to find someplace else to sleep that night. My roommate and I realized that there was some fun to be had at their expense. We arranged to leave one of their windows unlocked one day while we were in their room. Later, we climbed into their room from outside (don't ask), and put the chain lock on the door. Every day for three days, each one of them would come back to their dorm room and find that the chain lock was on. Each one of them thought that the other one was having the time of their lives. (Remember, this was before cell phones; now roommates can text each other, but not back then.) It took them three days to bump into each other on campus and realize that they had been pranked. It took them fifteen seconds to figure out who had done the pranking.

Toilet Ball, anyone?

* * * * *
I Killed a Newspaper Machine

I obtained my driving learners permit on December 29, 1977, my sixteenth birthday. My father took me out driving right away. We spent a few minutes practicing in a parking lot, and then he took me out on some quiet side streets in Northeast Philadelphia.

We were driving on St. Vincent Street, a few blocks from our home, and the traffic started to pick up. There was some two-way traffic, and cars were parked on both sides of the street. I thought the road was narrow and the driving was getting difficult, so my father asked me to turn onto a side street so that I could stop driving.

As we approached the corner where I was going to turn, there was a traffic light with a *Philadelphia Bulletin* newspaper machine chained to it. (The *Philadelphia Bulletin*'s motto was "nearly everyone reads the Bulletin." I guess not, because they went out of business many years ago.) I made my final approach for the right turn, and my father started yelling "too close—too close!" then I heard a crunch, and I saw the newspaper machine fly onto a neighborhood front lawn.

My father took over driving and drove us home. I was crushed. I was now the Worst Driver Ever. We went home, and I sulked off to my room, certain to never drive again.

About two hours later, my father came to my room and told me that he had our car repaired. He handed me the car keys, and said "let's go out driving again." His idea was "if you fall off a horse, get right back on the horse." Good move, Dad. I've driven for forty years without hitting anything else.

May that newspaper machine rest in peace . . .

* * * * *
Order! Order!

When I was young, I loved to open brand-new boxes of crayons. I loved the smell of the crayons and I loved the sharpener. I especially loved the organization of the box. Each crayon was perfect, and each row was perfectly aligned.

That love of order has carried over into my adult life. I subscribe to the "a place for everything, and everything in its place" school of thought. I keep things organized, I put things back, and I keep a lot of lists. I like order.

I am easily distracted, especially visually. I have a need to look at only one thing at a time. My desk is always clear, and so are my personal spaces, like my car and my bedside table. I have eliminated all of the clutter and distractions. I like orderly surroundings. My colleagues know this, and sometimes (just to tease me) they will move things around on my desk.

• • •

If you've ever had a toddler, or a puppy, or taken care of an ill relative, you know that it isn't always possible to keep things organized. I remember picking up little puzzle pieces and toys in my home for what seemed like decades when my daughters were young. There are dog toys all over my home right now (my dog doesn't have the same need for organization that I do).

Even if you are not organized, you want some people in your life to be very organized. You want your surgeon, your pilot, and your accountant to be organized. If you've ever read a story about a surgeon who left a surgical instrument inside a patient, or an accountant who forgot to file client income tax returns, you know what I mean.

There is a book about creating organization in important situations, called *The Checklist Manifesto*. It has great pointers for people who want (or need) more organization in their lives.

. . .

I married someone who is even more organized than I am. She would deny that, but she is highly organized. Because of her, bills are paid on time, birthdays are remembered, and appointments are kept. She is the glue that keeps our family life together.

I should take a moment to say how grateful I am for that. I am grateful for it because order means a lot to me. I experience order on a gut level. At the most basic level, my experience is "order=safety" and "chaos=danger." So I try to keep things as orderly as possible, for my own peace of mind.

. . .

M any years ago (before children), we lived in an apartment complex. There was a resident who lived in our building who would go out to the parking lot every day and sweep the parking lot. I used to call her "the Sweeper." I suppose it gave her some peace of mind to do that. I think she was trying to create some order out of chaos in her life.

I am reminded of the line in the movie *The Incredibles*, where Mr. Incredible says, "I just cleaned up this mess! Can we keep it clean for ten minutes?"

★ ★ ★ ★ ★
Beat the Traffic

I have experienced some incredible traffic jams.

On the way to a Grateful Dead concert (July 4, 1987), my friend Alan, Theresa, and I got caught in the mother of all traffic jams. We exited I-95 (about four miles from the stadium) five hours before show time. We did not make it to the stadium by show time. Traffic was so gridlocked that Alan had to pull over to the side of the road and park his car next to some trees near the highway. That seemed like a good idea while it was still light outside. After the show was over, we realized that we did not know where he was parked. I still think it is miraculous that we found his car.

One night after work (a Friday night, of course), there was an accident near the Pennsylvania Turnpike tollbooths that blocked all but one tollbooth from allowing cars through. Traffic was blocked for eight miles on southbound Route 1. Traffic was so bad on Route 1 South that some cars ran out of gas and had to be pushed to the side of the road. It took me four hours to get home that night. I never made it onto the turnpike. I had to take side roads to get home. Sixty miles of side roads. That is why I always use the restroom before I get into the car, and make sure that I have at least a half tank of gas.

After a Peter Frampton concert (June 11, 1977) at JFK Stadium, 110,000 concertgoers all tried to leave the area at the same time. Three hours later, we were still in a stadium parking lot with many of the 110,000 concertgoers. Some of them may still be there.

• • •

As a result of these (and many other) traffic disasters, I try to avoid traffic at all costs. I am obsessed about this. Whenever I attend sporting events and concerts, I start planning my exit strategy before the event begins.

I leave concerts at the beginning of the encore. I leave sporting events before everyone else. I am out of there. I take great pride in leaving before the traffic starts. Unfortunately, I sometimes miss greatness. I once missed Bruce Springsteen coming onstage to play at a U2 concert. I also have missed a couple of great sports comebacks.

But I don't care. I must beat the traffic.

• • •

"Beat the traffic" has become a running joke in my life. It is even going to be part of my funeral. At my funeral, my daughters are supposed to tell all of the attendees (thousands of them, no doubt) how obsessed I was about beating the traffic. Then they are supposed to tell all of the attendees that if they would like, they can all leave five minutes early to beat the traffic.

I won't be there anymore anyway ... I beat the traffic.

• • •

Thinking Out Loud, Part II

A Gordian Knot

I know a couple of people who are struggling with big life problems, including the loss of career (and the loss of income that goes along with a career), legal issues, financial issues, and relationship issues.

These people are in a place where they are struggling to find workable solutions. Every solution seems to have impossible challenges. Most of the solutions require some money (which requires a career and an income stream). If you lose your career and your income stream, you lose money, and then you lose a lot of options.

• • •

There is a legend called the "Gordian knot." A Gordian knot (according to Google) is named after Gordius, king of Gordium, who "tied an intricate knot and prophesied that whoever untied it would become the ruler of Asia. It was cut through with a sword by Alexander the Great." Other definitions of Gordian knots include an "intractable problem" or "impossible knot."

• • •

I have had some problems in my life that seemed impossible. When I was twenty-one, I was newly graduated from college with a mountain of debt and no career prospects. I had no meaningful relationship, no career, no real income stream, lots of debt, and no idea how to move my life forward.

I also had a failure of imagination. I thought that the way my life was at the age of twenty-one was the way it was going to be for the rest of my life. If you had told twenty-one-year-old me that I would be where I am right now, doing what I am doing, married to my best friend, with two wonderful daughters and the greatest dog in the world, I would have asked, "what kind of dog?" That is who I was back then. I focused on the problems, and lacked imagination. I lacked the imagination to believe that great things were possible in my life. I had no capacity to believe that something much better was in my future.

When Gordius asked someone to solve the problem of the knot, he thought that the only way to undo the knot was to untie it. Alexander didn't bother untying the knot; he cut through it instead.

I hope that I can help my friends cut through their knots instead of trying to untie them.

★ ★ ★ ★ ★

A Life Worth Living

A friend recently mentioned that she keeps a "Life Worth Living" list. She explained that it's a list of things in her life that make her life worth living, a list of the things in her life that are good and worthwhile. She goes back to the list from time to time to make sure that she is doing the things on her list that make her life worth living.

It isn't a list of "things I like to do" or "things that are pleasurable," although both of those are on her list. Her list is a list of "what gives my life meaning and purpose?"

• • •

What makes my life worth living? What follows is a very quick list. I haven't given this a lot of thought, so if there is something obvious missing from this, I will go back and add it . . .

1. Family time—I love our Sunday night dinners, our drives and walks together, and crossword puzzle time.
2. Meditation and prayer—I need time to reflect and refresh.
3. Exercise—I love to work out. I feel much better after I've completed a rigorous workout.
4. Work time—I love my work. The people that I work with are doing really important work. They are trying to find cures for some rare types of cancers. It is an honor to work with them.
5. Writing—I love to write. If I could write for a living, I would. I wouldn't mind having two full-time jobs at the same time!
6. Service time—I am on the board of directors of three non-profits. I read a blog by someone recently who said that his greatest joy in life was to be of service to others.
7. Beach time—I love the beach; I love the ocean. I also love crossword puzzle time with Theresa, and walks with my family, and taking Darwin to the park. Visits with my father and my in-laws, Eagles games and rock concerts with friends. ... all of this is "beach time."

I'm curious to hear what is on your list.

* * * * *

Who Do We Honor?

(I wrote this essay a few years ago, at a time when some war statues were being torn down or moved.)

I was walking through Philadelphia yesterday, and I passed a statue. Statues have been in the news a lot lately. Cities and towns all over the

United States are engaged in conversations about who is or isn't appropriate to be celebrated with a statue. I spent the rest of the day thinking about why we put people on statues, and what we are celebrating when we do.

We don't actually put up a lot of statues anymore. I can't remember the last time that I saw a statue commissioned and displayed. Instead, we put people on pedestals by wearing clothing with their names on the back, or the name of their band on the front. We celebrate athletes and rock stars, and we put them on pedestals.

Why is that?

• • •

A few years ago, I read a book called *Friday Night Lights*. It was written by Buzz Bissinger. Bissinger moved to Plano, Texas, and lived in the community of the high school football team. His book was an exposé of the high school football culture in that town.

Bissinger described the love affair that Plano had with their team. They adored the football team, and they put that team on a pedestal. They taught the team that the football players were above the rules that everyone else had to follow. The football players did not have to go to class or follow any of the rules that applied to the other students in that community.

What is remarkable about the book isn't that one town in Texas gets crazy about high school football players. What is remarkable is that so many towns get crazy about football players, basketball players, baseball players, and other athletes.

If we get that crazy about high school athletics, imagine what we do with college athletics. How many college athletes don't go to class? How many college athletes don't participate in college life, other than athletics?

Why is that?

• • •

Our culture celebrates athletes and musicians. These are people who know how to do one thing really well. It may be a three-point shot, a drum roll, a home run, or a guitar riff, but these stars have achieved expertise in doing one thing better than anyone else in the world.

What follows is just my opinion … In order to become the very best in the world at something, I believe that you have to make a choice to not learn how to do many other important things. If you spend years of your life trying to become the best outfielder or the best guitar player in the world, then you decide to not take the time to learn things that the rest of us have to learn. If you spend all of your time developing guitar skills, you have no time left to learn how to become a husband, or father, or citizen.

We know who the best guitar players and athletes are. Ask your friends who won the Super Bowl last year, or whose tour is sold out this year. They will know the answer. Ask your friends who the best teacher is at their local high school, or who the best cardiologist or oncologist is in their community, and they will not know. Your friends know the name of someone who can throw a football, but they won't know the names of people who have saved or changed hundreds of lives in their own community.

Why is that?

• • •

Why do we celebrate people who do a trivial thing exceptionally well but are often unable to live the rest of their lives successfully? Why don't we celebrate people who do vitally important things very well? We celebrate the guitar riff and the three-point shot, but not a well-organized teaching plan, effective first-responder training, or successful bypass surgery. Would you recognize the best pediatrician or teacher in your state if you saw them at the supermarket? Would you ask them for their autographs?

In my book *Can Openers*, I wrote an essay called "Role Models." Go purchase the book. I am donating all of the proceeds to Philadelphia-area charities. Or go find the essay on my website for free. Here is a spoiler alert about that essay: my role models aren't rock stars or athletes anymore. And if my interventional cardiologist ever has a T-shirt or jersey for sale, I will buy it.

* * * * *

Globalization

I once attended a wedding where the father of the bride noted that guests had traveled from twelve states and three countries to attend the wedding.

My daughter is leaving next week to study in Italy.

I'm going to Japan soon for business. It's the twentieth time I'll be going to Japan.

• • •

My father drove to the wedding with my family. He noted that his parents (my paternal grandparents) were never on an airplane. When his parents were growing up, "airports" weren't created yet. The Wright brothers' first flight took place only two years before my grandmother was born.

• • •

We have become a mobile society. I didn't know anyone who studied abroad when I went to college. My daughter knows dozens of people who have studied abroad. When I was young, I didn't know anyone who traveled outside of the United States, except for those who had served in the military. The first time I traveled abroad, I was in my late twenties. My wife and I had to scrimp and save for the trip. It seemed so exotic at the time.

My older daughter has been to twenty countries, my younger daughter to fifteen. They collect passport stamps like I used to collect baseball cards. Many of their friends are fortunate enough to do the same thing.

Both of my daughters have friends who have moved to other countries because their parents now work outside of the United States. I know two people who have purchased second homes in other countries. And I thought it was exotic to vacation in Atlantic City when I was young.

Twice this year we have mistakenly handed someone the wrong currency. If you hand someone euros and they are expecting pounds, be prepared for a terse "That's not my currency." Anytime someone makes a mistake in my house, the fastest way make them laugh is to say, "That's not my currency."

• • •

I was invited to a dinner in Japan about a year ago. The host of the dinner invited three of his friends to the dinner. The host and his three friends all joined the same company thirty-five years ago. They still work for the same company thirty-five years later.

I tried explaining to him that I don't know anyone who has worked for the same company for thirty-five years. I also tried explaining to him that I don't know anyone who knows four people who have worked together at the same company for thirty-five years. It is almost impossible for that to happen anymore. According to the Bureau of Labor Statistics, Baby Boomers held an average of 11.9 jobs between the ages of eighteen and fifty! (News Release, August 24, 2017). That means they will change jobs, on average, every three years between graduation and retirement. That is a lot of movement.

• • •

I think of the changes in transportation and society that have occurred between the time of my grandparents and me. I wonder what types of changes will happen between now and the time of my grandchildren. I wonder if they will be space tourists.

* * * * *

Making Mistakes

I learned early in life that making mistakes was a bad thing. I learned that making mistakes meant failure, and that mistakes should be avoided at all costs.

I learned that lesson so well that I became afraid to try new things. Why try something new if I was going to be bad (fail) at it?

Then I went to pharmacy school, and I was taught to avoid mistakes at all costs. A dispensing error had the potential to be fatal, and I didn't want to kill a patient.

What if everything I learned about making mistakes was wrong?

. . .

I started a new career in the pharmaceutical industry in 1994. Soon after I started in that career, the CEO of the company I was working for gave a talk at a company "all-hands" meeting. He said something that I'll never forget. "If you're not making mistakes, you're doing something wrong." I was shocked. He doubled down on what he said and continued with, "If you are not making mistakes, you are not trying hard enough."

Wow.

That was the first time someone ever encouraged me to make a mistake. I've never looked at mistakes the same way since.

. . .

While I was working at that same company, one of my colleagues and I were campaigning our boss to institute a double-checking feature on a certain part of our work.

He looked at one of us and he replied, "If you are double-checking the work," then he looked at the other one of us and continued, "and you are also double-checking the work," before looking at both of us and asking, "which one of you don't I need?"

Ouch.

He was right. My colleague and I were so focused on doing this task perfectly that we lost sight of the big picture. The task we were trying to perfect was okay being 99.5% correct. Trying to make it perfect was a waste of time and energy.

• • •

In the drug development arena, pharmaceutical companies have a 5–15% chance of obtaining a drug approval for a compound entering phase III clinical trials. There is an expression in this arena: "fail faster." It costs a lot of money to try to develop new drugs. The faster a company realizes that its compound isn't approvable, the faster it can stop development and move its resources toward a possibly more effective compound.

Imagine my reaction the first time someone told me to "fail faster."

• • •

Mark Twain supposedly said, "Good decisions come from experience. Experience comes from making bad decisions."

Hopefully I am making more good decisions than bad ones. But I am not afraid of making mistakes anymore.

★ ★ ★ ★ ★

Missing

(This was originally published on halwardblog.com on March 30, 2015.)

On my drive into work, there is a telephone pole with a sign attached that says, "Missing Parrot." The sign has a photo of the parrot. The sign is laminated and has been stapled to this telephone pole for years. Sometimes I see the sign, and I wonder where the parrot went.

• • •

On March 8, 2014, Malaysian Airlines 370 (MH370), a Boeing 777, took off from Kuala Lumpur. It never arrived in Beijing. Searchers have found relatively few pieces of the airplane.

Where did MH370 go?

• • •

In the past four months, I have read news stories about four people who went missing, three of them with local connections.

Just before Thanksgiving, a student from West Chester University went missing. His body was recovered several weeks later near the Schuykill River.

I used to work at a pharmacy with another pharmacist. His twenty-two-year-old son, a nurse in Pittsburgh, went missing during the Christmas holidays. Search parties were formed, but he has not been located.

And most recently, a local thirteen-year-old boy went missing for several days. Search parties were formed. His body was found. Tragically, he committed suicide.

• • •

After the attacks of September 11, Bruce Springsteen wrote a song called "You're Missing." I listened to it this week.

• • •

I work with a couple of local charities and non-profit organizations that try to help struggling people get back on their feet. I had been working with three different men. I knew their names, addresses, phone numbers, and their email addresses. I was getting to know each of them. I listened to their hopes and dreams, their fears and their worries.

All three have disappeared. They moved, I think, and they didn't respond to telephone calls, email, or text messages.

Where did they go?

• • •

When I went to school, the teacher used to do roll call.. Roll call was taking attendance. I didn't even see it sometimes. Because we had assigned seats, the teacher only had to look for empty seats, and knew immediately who was not there that day.

• • •

When I was growing up, I sometimes went to public swimming pools. The lifeguards used the buddy system. Every child was assigned a buddy. I was supposed to stay close to my buddy, and if the lifeguard blew the whistle, my buddy and I were supposed to hold our hands together up high to show the lifeguard that we were present and accounted for. Anyone without a buddy was supposed to make a lot of noise.

• • •

I have a couple of relatives who are estranged from our extended family. One left over thirty years ago, and has not been heard from since. Where did they go? Why are they missing?

* * * * *

I ask a lot of questions.

I ask those questions to try to make sense of the world. I write this blog to help with that, too.

Sometimes things happen that make no sense to me at all. And no matter how many times I ask "why?" I can't find an answer that makes sense.

So I hug my wife and my girls and my dog, and I thank God my family is with me today.

All present and accounted for.

* * * * *

In Ten Years

In the book *The 7 Habits of Highly Effective People*, Stephen R. Covey suggests to "begin with the end in mind." He suggests that the reader should write their own eulogy as a set of long-term goals. In other words, if you think about what your long-term goals are, you are more likely to achieve them. If you want your eulogy to say that you were a world-class violin player, it might be time to go purchase a violin and take some lessons.

• • •

I just celebrated my fifty-sixth birthday. My late-December birthday gives me the chance to take some time off and reflect on my life. I thought about what my life might be like in ten years.

My wife will be sixty-five in ten years. She wants to retire, hopefully sooner instead of later, and then travel the world together. We are saving for retirement aggressively. With a little luck, in ten years she will be planning another month in Europe for us, and trying to help us complete the Seven Continent Challenge. In the next ten years, we will travel to Australia, Africa, and Latin America, and will complete the Seven Continent Challenge with a cruise to Antarctica. (With any luck, we will squeeze in a holiday in an overwater bungalow.) We have filled three passports. We have three more to fill. I mean that.

My children will probably be moving out in the next ten years. My older daughter will probably get an apartment soon, and my younger daughter wants to go away to school. In as little as twenty months, my wife and I may be empty nesters, at least part of the time.

My children will complete their college education in the next ten years. My wife and I hope to help them complete that education without any school loans. With any luck, maybe one of them will have little urchins. Which means grandurchins for me to play with. We'll see.

My family: My father is eighty-five, my in-laws are in their late eighties, and I have aunts and uncles in their nineties. My dear friend Bill is in his late eighties. I don't know how many of them will be alive in ten years. Maybe some of them, and maybe none of them. Every time I see them, I make it a point to soak up every bit of our time together. The truth is that they won't be here forever, and neither will I.

Darwin: The greatest dog in the world, and this man's second-best friend, won't be here in ten years. I hate to write that, but he is currently probably eight years old or so. (When you rescue a homeless dog, you don't know exactly how old it is.) My time with Darwin is limited. Every time we go to Darwin Park—you'll read more about the park later in this book—I try to remember that someday I will be wishing for one more walk around the park with him.

My heart: I have two stents in my left anterior descending artery (LAD), also known as the "widow-maker." If either of those stents closes off completely, I have four minutes of life left. I take my exercise seriously. My total cholesterol is lower than yours (average about 110), my blood pressure is probably lower than yours (average 115/75), and my heart rate is in the 50s. If I want to be around in ten years (and I do—I have three passports to fill and four grandurchins to play with), I have to be very serious about this part of my life. My spin instructors see me four times a week, and I intend to continue that (or similar) for the rest of my life.

My Work: I hope to continue working, and be working in ten years. Not for money, but for fun and a sense of meaning and purpose. One of my friends talks about us having an "expiration date" in the workplace. I knew what he meant the first time he said it. I want to extend my expiration date as long as possible.

Book Five: In ten years, I hope to publish my fifth book. I love to write, and I intend to do so all of the days of my life.

• • •

The point of writing this down for me is to set goals, and also to share it, and hopefully inspire someone else to do the same. For my family and friends, please let me know what you hope to be doing in ten years.

★ ★ ★ ★ ★

Give Me a Choice

I don't like to be told what to do. I don't react well when someone points a finger at me and orders me to do something. My first reaction is either "no" or "why?" My sense is that this is a universal reaction. The people I know react badly to orders.

On the other hand, I do react well to requests. If someone asks me for my help, or they ask me if I am willing to do something, I usually say yes. I want to help other people. I react better to the gesture of someone reaching out their hand for help, instead of the gesture of pointing a finger at me.

• • •

When I was young, I was introduced to the Ten Commandments. What I took away from my first experience with the commandments was a sense of finger pointing. I had a difficult time getting past the "Thou shalt" and the "Thou shalt not."

I recently read an essay by someone who noted that he would have reacted better to the commandments if they had been written a bit more gently. In other words, instead of "Honor thy father and thy mother," perhaps something like "We honored our fathers and our mothers." Instead of "Thou shalt remember the Sabbath day," perhaps "We remembered the Sabbath day."

The act of sharing experience ("this is what we did") is easier for me to accept than being told what to do ("do this or else").

This concept works for me in parenting and in personal relationships. When I ask my children and my family for help, help is always available. When I point fingers and try to boss them around, I don't get very good results.

• • •

If some of what I have just written seems like I have a problem with authority, I suppose that is true. I just looked up a definition of authority, and the definition was "the power or right to give orders, make decisions, or enforce obedience."

My first reaction to the idea of someone enforcing obedience or giving orders is, "Who put you in charge of me?"

I grew up learning about the American Revolution and the Declaration of Independence. It sounds like my American ancestors weren't happy about being told what to do, either.

Where I come from, respect for authority is earned, not automatically granted. Respect for authority is based on trust, and that trust can be lost a lot easier than it can be gained.

* * * * *

Don't Wait Until the Last Minute

When I was in college, there was a fellow who lived next door to me who had exceptional study habits. He would study rigorously, and he made it look easy. He organized his time, and he studied (almost) every night. He began studying for exams weeks in advance. He blocked his time into manageable periods, and he used each period for a different task.

The night before a big exam, he had a "cutoff time." He would stop studying by 7 p.m. or so, go out for some pizza and a beer, and then get a full night of sleep. He was taking a difficult engineering curriculum, and his grade point average was a 4.0. I sometimes asked him about his "pizza and a beer" routine. He explained that he would study in advance for an exam, and an extra hour or two of studying the night before would not make a difference.

By contrast, I would start studying around the same time that he was going out for his pizza and a beer. My grade point average was less than his 4.0. A lot less.

I met with a counselor at that college, and she explained to me that I ought to be studying for two hours for every hour of class that I had. In other words, if I was taking sixteen credits (sixteen hours of class a week), I ought to be studying for thirty-two hours a week. I was shocked at the suggestion.

I later had the opportunity to pursue a second degree and a third degree, and when I did, I applied the "two hours of studying per hour of class" rule to my curriculum. I planned my studying times a week in advance on my calendar. My grade point average rose to a 4.0. Not a surprise.

I have shared this experience with my daughters, and anyone else who will listen. Now I'm sharing it with you. I don't wait until the last minute.

• • •

This approach to studying works well in other areas of my life. One area is saving for retirement. I cannot expect to save for retirement if I "wait until the night before the exam." I have to plan ahead, and put money away every week, if I want to have retirement savings.

• • •

I spoke to someone recently about the idea of waiting until the last minute.. This fellow has a problem with being late. He is late for work, he is late for family functions, he is late for a lot of things. He is so late for so many things that it is starting to cost him.

His approach to attending things is that he looks at the deadline and works backward in order to determine how much time it will take to get to the place he has to go to. He doesn't leave any extra time for traffic, unexpected delays, etc. He does not plan in advance.

• • •

I recently read a book called *Habit Stacking: 127 Small Changes to Improve Your Health, Wealth, and Happiness* by S.J. Scott. The author shares his strategies for incorporating healthy habits into his life.

One of the things he discusses at length is the concept of "keystone habits." Keystone habits are those habits that are so good for us that they have ripple effects into other areas of our lives. Rigorous exercise is a keystone habit. People who have an exercise program tend to eat better, sleep better, and lose weight—all as a result of exercising. As a result of starting an exercise program, they improve multiple areas of their lives.

The author also discusses the strategy of "supporting habits." He notes that if you want to implement a keystone habit (like exercise) into your life, you should support that effort with other habits. He suggests packing a bag the day before you exercise (with exercise clothes, water bottle, and other appropriate supplies) so that when it is time to go exercise, the bag is already packed. Packing an exercise bag in advance eliminates the excuse of "I didn't pack my bag, and I don't have enough time to do so."

• • •

I mentioned earlier the book called *The Checklist Manifesto* by Atul Gawande. The author wrote about how important checklists are for important things in life. He shared examples of surgeons who use checklists in the operating room, and airline pilots who use checklists in the cockpit.

I started using checklists in my life several years ago. When I walk into work on Monday morning, I have a checklist of things I must do between 7 and 9 a.m. I block my calendar, and I complete those tasks.

I also have a packing-list checklist. Several years ago, I wrote down everything that I need for a trip (business or personal). When it is time for me to pack, I print a copy of the list, and I pack everything that I need. I never forget anything, and because of the checklist, I don't have to remember anything, either.

And I don't wait until the last minute to use that checklist.

★ ★ ★ ★ ★
Moving Parts

(This was originally published on August 25, 2015 on halwardblog.com.)

I have observed or experienced several transitions recently. They include the following:

My younger daughter graduated from middle school and is about to start high school.

She finished her club volleyball season and just had tryouts for high school volleyball.

My older daughter spent the summer working in Manhattan (her first extended stay away from home), and received an internship offer for next summer already. A full-time offer is likely if she does well next summer. And she just started her junior year in college.

One of our neighbors moved away, due to a work relocation.

The fellow who sat next to me at work moved back to Japan. Two more colleagues just resigned.

Our water heater broke, and we had to repair a lot of damage in the basement.

My favorite band retired.

We did a lot of travel in the last six weeks. I've been to Japan, New Orleans, Chicago, Japan again, and Turks and Caicos. All good stuff, but a lot of travel.

I just started an exercise class.

And on a somber note, a couple of good friends are battling serious illnesses.

That is a lot of moving parts.

* * * * *

My Identity Cannot Be Stolen

Some years ago there was news coverage about a security breach at Equifax. 143 million people may have had some of their personal information stolen, including credit card numbers, social security numbers, and passwords.

I have experienced "identity theft" twice. It isn't fun. It also isn't surprising, because my social security number is everywhere. It exists in databases and files with every credit bureau, mortgage company, credit card company, medical practice, insurance company, and employer that I've interacted with.

If you don't have my social security number, you aren't trying hard enough. Everyone else already has it.

• • •

Many years ago, my wife and I were at a shopping mall doing some holiday shopping. When we left the mall, we walked back to our car in the parking lot. I pulled out my keys, and went to unlock the car, but the car was not there anymore.

It was stolen.

• • •

As I mentioned earlier, when I published my first book (*Can Openers: Essays about Life and Love*) I decided I would donate all of the proceeds from the sale of my book to Philadelphia-area charities. I've made donations to TE Care and Broad Street Ministry.

About a week after my book was published, PDF copies started appearing for sale on the internet. Back then, if you ran an internet search on "Hal Ward Can Openers," on the first page you would find a couple of links for PDF copies of my book. I didn't authorize those. That's okay though. If someone wanted my book that much, I am glad that they read it.

If you would like a copy of my book, and you don't want to pay for it, send me a note at halward@comcast.net. I'll give you my address. If you send me a self-addressed mailer, I will send you a signed copy of my book. In return I ask that you make a donation to your favorite charity in your community.

I'm serious about that. If you want to read my book, then I want you to read it too. It reflects who I am, what I think, and what I believe in.

It represents my identity. It represents me.

• • •

My credit information has been compromised.
My car has been stolen.
My book has been copied.
So what?

I have heard the term "identity theft" used a hundred times this month. I think that is a misnomer. My credit information and my car can be stolen, but my identity can never be taken from me. That will always be mine, and mine alone.

* * * * *
I'm Voting

(This was originally published on April 25, 2016 on halwardblog.com.)

(I wrote this before an election, about the importance of participating in our democracy.)

* * * * *
A few facts about our election system:

There are currently 319 million people living in the United States. As of 2012 (the last presidential election), 235 million people were eligible to vote (they were over the age of 18, and were citizens of the US). Of those, 129 million people voted in the 2012 presidential election. In other words, 54.9% of the eligible voters actually voted. Of those, the victor (President Obama) received about 65 million votes.

That means that for every 100 people living in the US, only 20 voted for the President.

• • •

There are about 12.5 million people living in Pennsylvania. In 2012, there were 8.5 million registered voters in Pennsylvania. In 2012, only 20% of eligible voters voted in the Pennsylvania primary election. That means about 1.7 million people voted in the 2012 Pennsylvania primary election—1.7 million voters.

Half of that about 850,000 people) would form a majority of voters. In a state of 12.5 million people.

• • •

Let's put that in perspective. Imagine a group of 125 people who are trying to make a decision. Seventeen take part in a vote. Nine vote for the winning side.

That decision represents the will of 125 people.

• • •

It is ridiculous that nine people are allowed to decide what happens to 125 people. But since I have a choice, I am going to be one of those nine people tomorrow.

I don't understand why some people are not registered to vote. I also don't understand why some people are registered to vote, and don't vote.

I'm voting tomorrow.

★ ★ ★ ★ ★
I Would Like to Speak to Customer Service

Once when my family was waiting at the gate for a flight in Europe, an airline representative made an announcement in the local language, and all of the local people left their seats and started to walk away quickly. I walked up to the airline representative, and she said that the flight had been canceled.

The airline never rebooked us. We stayed at the airport for three hours just to retrieve our bags from the plane. We had to make separate arrangements on our own in order to fly home, on another airline.

There are laws in Europe that protect passengers in this situation. Passengers are entitled to compensation for canceled and delayed flights, as long as certain conditions are met. We met those conditions. But the airline avoided payment for two months.

• • •

M ore recently, I scheduled an appointment with a service company that never showed up at our home, although we had a scheduled time. I tried calling for two weeks to reschedule the appointment, but they never returned my calls. This is a company that doesn't get paid if they don't show up. They didn't show up.

• • •

M y wife and I worked with a home technology company to try to reset a password. The company could not seem to do this. We tried to reset it for two months. It was their technology—why couldn't they reset their password?

• • •

W hat has happened to customer service, especially at large companies? I know that customer service representatives don't "make money" for a large company the same way that salespeople do. For companies that get paid every month (cable, internet, utilities), it seems like the customer service calculation is "how bad can we make customer service and still keep most of our customers?"

• • •

C ustomer service has gotten so bad that I remember the exceptions, when customer service is good. A few recent examples:
1. I took my car to the dealer for a minor repair. They didn't charge me for the work, because they said I am a frequent and loyal customer.
2. My family and I took a trip on a small "upstart" airline. I needed boarding passes, and we didn't have accounts with the airline. I

called their customer service. Within five minutes I was speaking to a representative who told me that she could email me the boarding passes. While I was on the phone with her I received them.

3. We work with a general contractor and an electrician, and we love to work with them. They deliver high-quality work, on budget.

Why can't every company deliver high-quality customer service?

* * * * *

Dress Codes

One day while driving my daughter to school, we talked about dress codes. Her school didn't have a dress code, and it didn't need one. Everyone dressed the same, whether they thought so or not. Well, almost everyone. She told me that two students wore capes to school every day. They were going through a goth stage.

That reminded me of the scene in the movie *The Incredibles* where Edna, the costume designer for the Incredibles family, refused to design costumes with capes. "No capes!" she said. She explained that capes could get caught in propellers. I guess there are no propellers at our local high school, so the students could wear capes.

• • •

I have a dress code. I wear button-down shirts and chinos to work every day. No one makes me do that. It's comfortable, and appropriate for where I work. Every shirt that I have is either blue or white (with checks or stripes sometimes), and every pair of pants is either tan, brown, or black. So I don't have to think about what I am wearing in the morning. I just grab a shirt and a pair of pants, and I'm off to work. I could get dressed in the dark (sometimes I do, at four a.m.), and it doesn't matter.

• • •

I read that Steve Jobs wore a black T-shirt and black pants every day. He didn't want to make any choices about what he wore, because he felt that that was a waste of "choice energy." He wanted to reserve all of his energy for choices that he felt were more important.

• • •

In Japan, every April 1 is New Hire Day. Japanese companies hire classes of new university graduates, and they all start on April 1. Do a search for photos of "Japanese New Hire Day." All of the entering employees dress exactly alike.

There seems to be a cultural aversion to being different there. They have an expression (I'm paraphrasing here), "tall trees get blown over by the wind." It means that those who stand out get knocked over. It isn't appropriate there to "stand out."

• • •

I guess no one wears a cape on New Hire Day there.

• • •

FAMILY & FRIENDS

My Mother's Day Card

In 2004, I was on a business trip in London. In the middle of my trip, I received a note: "CALL HOME—URGENT." I called Theresa, and she told me the bad news. My mother had had a stroke, and I needed to get onto the next plane home. The next plane home wasn't until the following morning. I rushed from the plane to the hospital to see my mom.

Before they would let me see her, the neurologist spoke to me, in order to prepare me for what was ahead. He explained that she had had a devastating stroke, that she had lost one third of her brain function. She would never be the same again, and there was nothing that they could do about it.

I walked in the room to see her, and she was sitting up in bed talking to visitors. I was confused. There was a disconnect between what the neurologist prepared me for, and what I was seeing in front of me. I eventually learned that the neurologist was right. She had had a devastating stroke, and she never was the same again. While she could sit up in bed and talk to people, she lost most of her short-term memory. She could remember little details from years ago, but could not remember the name of someone she was just introduced to. She could recognize my face, but she had no idea what my name was.

She lost the ability to walk. Her legs could move, but she could not (or would not) walk. It was as if she forgot how to. And she had almost no interest in relearning. Therapists worked intensively with her, trying to help her to regain the ability, but she showed no interest. So she spent the rest of her days in a wheelchair or in bed.

She also lost her "filter." It is hard to explain, but I guess we all have a capacity to think inappropriate things, but not say them. My mother lost that capacity. Anything that she thought, she said. Some of it was surprising, some of it was shocking, and some of it hurt.

• • •

My father tried to care for my mother at home for almost a year. He was saintly about it, but after a year, he and my aunts found a wonderful nursing home for her. I know that might sound strange to some people, but it was a wonderful place. It was light, and warm, and clean, and it even smelled okay—something that doesn't always happen with nursing homes.

I visited her as much as I could, which was at least once a week. I would stop in, and we would have awkward conversations. I would feel bad before I went, and feel bad while I was there, and then feel bad on the way home. But I visited every week.

I started talking about this with some of my friends. One of them, a lady named Debbie, asked me about my mother every time she saw me. Debbie was a friend, she was our caterer, and she was a character. She had a 10,000-watt personality. She met my mother at a party that she catered for us. Debbie would come up to me every time that she saw me, squeeze my cheeks in her hands and say "Hey, dollface! How is your mother doing?"

• • •

In August 2008 I received a telephone call and learned that Debbie had been murdered by an ex-boyfriend. I miss Debbie. I never had the chance to tell her how much it meant to me that she asked me about my mother every time she saw me.

Six weeks after Debbie was murdered, my mother had a heart attack, and died on October 2, 2008. I had the chance to say goodbye to her and tell her that I loved her. I am grateful for that.

I think about my mother often. When I think of my mother, I often think of Debbie, who took it upon herself to ask me about my mother every time that she saw me.

I like to think that when my mother died, Debbie was waiting in heaven to greet her with a big hug and say, "Welcome to heaven, dollface!"

• • •

I go to the cemetery a few times a year. My mother and my grandmothers are buried next to each other. I stop by to say hello to my mom and to my grandmothers, Nettie and Helen. I'm named after Helen, so I say hello to her on behalf of myself, and also on behalf of Howard, Heather and Henry. Lots of people were named after her. (For reasons I do not understand, my grandfathers are buried in other cemeteries. It's complicated.)

I stop by to pay my respects and to tell them how we are all doing. I tell them about what my wife and my daughters are up to. My mother and my grandmothers would be so proud of them.

• • •

Mother's Day is a painful holiday for me. I don't have a mother anymore. I just have memories.

Mother's Day was weird for me for several years while my mother was still alive. Her body was still there, but most of what made her my mother was lost with the stroke.

I saw a photo of my mother recently, from a time before her stroke. I had forgotten what she looked like when she was standing up. Most of my memories of her are from after her stroke.

Mother's Day is a Norman Rockwell-type of a holiday for a lot of families. If you have read this far, you can tell that it isn't that way for me. It is a sad day for me. I try to do my best as a husband and a father to make Mother's Day happy for my wife and my mother-in-law. But the truth is that my heart isn't into it sometimes. What I think about is ... even though the last several years of her life were tragic, even though I have a lot of painful memories . . .

I miss my mom.

* * * * *

The American Dream

There is a concept in American culture called the American Dream. It's hard to explain in words, but it means something like "be able to do and experience more than your parents did."

My wife and I have been incredibly lucky. We have been able to do and experience more than our parents did. In large part we have been able to do this because of our parents. Our parents sacrificed and provided for us in a way that is hard to describe.

As I write this, a word pops into my head: opportunity. We have, and have had, great opportunity available to us.

But the idea of the American Dream has changed.

• • •

There are a lot of reasons for that. Some of the opportunities that my wife and I were interested in (purchasing a home) don't seem to be as interesting to young people now. It may be because of the mortgage meltdown a few years ago, or the sagging real estate market, but young people are now more likely to rent apartments than they are to purchase homes. I haven't heard a young person speak about planning to purchase a home in a long time.

Another opportunity that is changing is employment. My parents expected lifetime employment. They finished their schooling, and sought employment with a company that they expected would take care of them for the rest of their lives. When my wife and I began life in the work world, we didn't expect lifelong employment, but we did expect full-time employment. Now young people do not necessarily want that. More young people are getting "contractor" roles, where their jobs are more like "gigs."

• • •

The American Dream, the idea of "doing better than your parents did," isn't possible for a lot of people right now. I listened to an interview with Bruce Springsteen during which he discussed "the difference between the American Dream and the American reality," and I understood what he meant.

Because of the expense of a college education, the expense of housing, and a lack of employment opportunity, many young people don't have the same kinds of opportunities that their parents had.

At the same time, I have to remember that my daughters don't want my dreams and opportunities. They want their own dreams and opportunities. The things that I dreamed of in 1970 are not the same things that they dream of now.

What I hope to do is to give them the opportunities to make their dreams come alive. If I can do that, then I am living the American Dream.

★ ★ ★ ★ ★
The Mazel Tov Guy

I wish my friends "mazel tov" a lot.

"Mazel tov" is a Yiddish phrase derived from the Hebrew words mazel (fortune) and tov (good). The expression means "good luck." It also means congratulations.

Think about that for a second. The expression actually means two things. It means congratulations for what has already happened, and good luck for what is yet to come. I like the sentiment of that. Saying "mazel tov" to someone is like a double blessing.

Most of my friends are not Jewish, but they don't mind when I sprinkle a little bit of Yiddish in our conversation. One of my friends recently called me "the mazel tov" guy.

You can do a lot worse in life than being known as the mazel tov guy.

* * * * *

My Great Depression Story

I know a couple who lived through the Great Depression. One of them did not have a winter coat as a child, and was unable to go outside for recess at school during the winter. They still save and reuse things like aluminum foil, and they don't waste a bit of food. Everything is eaten, nothing is wasted.

I have a Great Depression Story too. It didn't happen during the 1930s, but it is just as meaningful to me.

• • •

When I was in pharmacy school in 1985, I had a job working at Thomas Jefferson University Hospital as a pharmacy intern. If I worked a shift on a holiday weekend, one of the perks was a meal card at the hospital cafeteria. I would get my free meal (cheese fries and a soda), and that was my big meal for that day. That meal card was one of the reasons I took those holiday weekend shifts. I had nothing at the time, and a free meal was a big deal for me.

One summer during pharmacy school, I had two full-time jobs at the same time, while taking a course in biochemistry. That's right—I worked eighty hours a week in order to save for tuition, and I took a really difficult class. I had no money, and I was at risk of not being able to pay my pharmacy-school tuition.

After I graduated from pharmacy school, Theresa and I moved in together. It was 1988, and we still had nothing. I had just graduated from pharmacy school, and my net worth was a big red number (including about $20,000 in school loans, which is like $100,000 in school loans today). We found an apartment that was convenient for both of our jobs, and we moved in. We had an option to rent a one- or two-bedroom apartment. The two-bedroom apartment was an extra $25 a month, and we could not afford that, so we rented the one-bedroom apartment.

We could not afford furniture when we moved to this apartment. We had no bed, no box spring, and no mattress. For the first couple of months, we slept on the floor of our apartment in a sleeping bag. Once we could afford a mattress, we purchased it—but without a box spring or a bedframe. We only purchased what we could afford to pay cash for, so we did without things that people normally have in their homes and apartments.

We learned some important lessons in those years. One lesson we learned was how to do without things that we wanted, like furniture. We learned some other lessons, too.

• • •

We made career changes: When we first started dating, we were both working for the federal government. I was working in a research lab, and Theresa was working for a division of the US Navy. Both were worthwhile jobs, but they didn't pay well and did not have a career path. Within a year or two of meeting each other, I started pharmacy school, and Theresa transitioned into the financial sector.

Those risks paid off. It is now almost thirty years later, and our combined income is about thirteen times what it was then. Each one of us has had two career changes. We took career risks, and those risks paid off.

• • •

79

We invested in our education: We both come from families that consider an education the greatest gift that can be given to someone. Theresa has multiple certifications in her field, and I have three degrees. Theresa works for a company that educates and trains its employees, and she takes advantage of that.

• • •

We became ruthless savers: We save about 20% of our pre-tax income, or about 40% of our after-tax income. I use the word "ruthless" because that means that we make choices. Every decision that we make is a choice.

For example, we choose to drive well-used cars. Our cars have more than 400,000 miles on them. I want shiny new cars, but Theresa reminds me that that is a bad idea. Our cars are nothing more than tools that we use to move around.

We save because we never know what we are going to need and when we are going to need it. We also save because we remember what it is like to have nothing at all, and we don't want to go back there.

We learned to invest wisely and fearlessly: We keep our investing costs at zero. We don't pay for unneeded financial advice, we don't pay any brokers or advisers, and we don't pay any commissions. We haven't spent any money on commissions or fees in over a decade.

I'm going to borrow a marketing line from the company my wife works for: "Costs Matter." They really do. I know people who give away 1-5% of their portfolio every year on commissions and fees, in an attempt to "beat the market." That means they pay thousands of dollars a year for this. Instead of paying other people to invest my money, I keep it and invest it myself.

I have a secret to share with you: Theresa and I are the market that other people are trying to beat. We invest in ultra-low-cost mutual funds (like S&P 500 funds). We don't pay any fees or commissions to do so. Our taxes are deferred until we retire.

You cannot beat the market over time. You may be able to beat the market for a year or two if you're lucky, but you're just lucky. I encourage you to be the market, keep your costs at a minimum, and reap the rewards over time.

We learned that our house is not an investment: Our house is where we live, but it is not an investment. In spite of what you may have been told, houses do not appreciate much in value over time, after inflation. Don't believe me?

Exercise one: Take the purchase price of your home. Add in what you pay in real estate taxes every year. Add what you pay in maintenance every year. Add what you've paid for upgrades. Now look up the current estimated price for your home. Deduct the costs of real estate taxes, maintenance costs, and upgrades since you've purchased your house. Calculate the annual gain. Now compare that annual gain to the annual rate of inflation.

Not much difference, is there? The idea that "houses will always go up in value" isn't true. Find a chart that shows the inflation-adjusted price of houses, and it looks flat over time. A lot of people make money from the myth that houses are great investments. Real estate agents, mortgage companies, contractors, furniture and appliance companies, banks and lenders. No one is paid to tell the truth about the value of housing.

Exercise two: Still don't believe me about housing value? Find a one-percenter. Ask them what the source of their wealth is. It isn't their house.

We are incredibly lucky: We are not "self-made." We received an education, and great parenting, from our parents. Our parents taught us really important values, both in word and in deed.

We also have been very lucky in many of our choices. We changed careers, and those changes worked out well. But there are no guarantees in life; sometimes changes don't work well.

We have really good employers. Both of us work for companies, and people, who care about us and our families. So far, we have been able to work all of the days of our lives. We are healthy enough to do so, and we have employment that is rewarding and challenging.

We know that we aren't responsible for any of that. We both know people who work just as hard, and are very good and decent people, but they have not been as lucky as us.

We recycle, reuse, and repair: And at least one night a week, dinner is Leftover Night. Very little goes to waste. Not for someone who lived on cheese fries.

We don't forget where we came from: Theresa and I had nothing at all. We come from families that had to scrape just to get by. We try not to forget where we come from.

We give our time and our money to organizations that help people in need. We like organizations that combine "feed a man a fish" (help someone right now) with "teach a man to fish" (help someone help themselves, so that they can help someone else later on).

We remember who we are, where we are now, and where we were thirty years ago.

Sleeping in a sleeping bag.

★ ★ ★ ★ ★

Per Lui

(I wrote this essay some years ago, when my daughter was studying abroad in Milan, Italy).

I visited my daughter in Milan a couple of months ago. If you had told me twenty-five years ago that I would ever write the sentence "I visited my daughter in Milan," I would have laughed at you. At that point in my life, children weren't on the horizon, and even if I had had a child, why would that child be in another country?

But we did have a daughter (actually two, if I remember correctly), and one of them studied abroad in Milan. I never knew anyone who studied abroad when I was in college. It wasn't popular then. When I was twenty-one, I was more interested in going to rock concerts and trying not to get into too much trouble.

I met some of my daughters' friends while I was visiting her in Milan. Her friends are really intelligent, and really brave souls. They are scientists, businesspeople, and musicians. They have immersed themselves in Italian culture and Italian society. Some of them live with host families, and others live in off-campus housing. They know as much about living in Milan as some of the native Milanese. They have memorized the metro and tram systems, and they know where to find the best gelato, espresso, and pizza.

Have you ever heard older people say, "What's wrong with young people nowadays?" I can tell you what's right about young people nowadays. They are ten years ahead of where I was at the same age.

• • •

If you have children, you want the best for them. You want them to be healthy, happy, and independent. You want them to grow up to be independent, productive adults.

Sometimes when I see it happen, though, it seems bittersweet. There is this feeling of "that happened really quickly—where did the time go?"

• • •

I met my daughter in Milan, and I could tell right away that she had been changed by the experience. She looked more grown up, more mature, more confident.

As we left the hotel the first day, she turned to me, and she said, "Follow me." And then she did something really remarkable. She spoke only Italian in public for the next three days. She led us through Milan and Venice, through trains, cathedrals, museums and public spaces, and spoke to the local people in Italian.

How did that happen? When did my baby grow up?

● ● ●

Several times she ordered tickets and meals for me. Each time, she used the expression "per lui." I assumed that "per" in Italian was like "père" in French, which means "father." But I couldn't figure out why she was calling me "Father Louie." She wasn't. "Per lui" in Italian means "for him." She was ordering things for me, and said "for him, he will have ..."

I usually end my blog with my given name. This time I think I will sign off as . . .

Father Louie

★ ★ ★ ★ ★
The Smell of Popcorn

I walked into the house the other day, and I smelled popcorn. That popcorn smell reminded me of a certain leisure activity, and where that activity occurs, and then I thought about how amazing it is that one smell can trigger all of those thoughts.

I associate the smell of popcorn with going to the movies. I thought about going to the old Tyson Theater (the Castor and the Benner were also options in my youth). I thought about sitting in those old-fashioned movie houses, with popcorn and Milk Duds and not having a care in the world.

All because of one smell.

● ● ●

There are other smells that take me way back. I love the smell of chocolate chip cookies. When I smell that smell, I think "all is well." When my mother made chocolate chip cookies, it meant that life was good. I still have that feeling when I smell chocolate chip cookies.

There are other smells that bring that good feeling. The smell of cook-outs and burning leaves are really positive for me. They remind me that people spend time outdoors with their families and friends.

The smell of my wife's favorite perfume is a great smell. That smell means life is good. It means that we are dressing up and going out, and all is well in the world.

The smell of the ocean is like that, too. I can smell the ocean before I ever see it. That salt-water smell reminds me of vacations and beaches and sunshine. I love that smell.

• • •

But not every smell brings back that "life is good" feeling. Some smells remind me of sad times.

There is a smell in nursing homes and hospitals. That smell reminds me of my grandmother, and some of her end-of-life times. That smell is burned into my brain.

When I was in elementary school, the school custodian had this stuff that I used to call "puke powder." Anytime a student vomited, the custodian came around with this yellow powder which soaked up the vomit. It was sort of like a HazMat scene. There was a chemical in that powder that I still smell from time to time. Whenever I smell that chemical, it takes me right back to Solis-Cohen Elementary School.

Medicine has smells, too. Anytime I smell grape juice, I think of the grape flavor in cough syrup. The smell of bubble gum reminds me of liquid antibiotics that my children had to take.

• • •

Why do smells have such powerful effects? I can't think of sounds or tastes or touches that evoke those kinds of reactions in me.

I want some chocolate chip cookies . . .

* * * * *
Comfortable in My Own Skin

(This was originally published on May 26, 2016, on halwardblog.com.)

About fifteen years ago, I had a physician's appointment. My physician was looking at my back, and she said, "I don't like the looks of this." I asked her what she meant, and she told me that she saw a spot on my skin that looked abnormal. She referred me to a dermatologist.

I went to the dermatologist, and he looked at the spot, and he agreed that he didn't like the look of it. He did a "whole body" check, and he found nine more spots that he also didn't like. He removed all of them, biopsied them, and they all came back as non-cancerous.

He suggested that I should be examined every six months, because of the number of moles and pigmented spots that I have on my body. I do see him every six months for routine checks. Twice he has biopsied something and discovered that it was pre-cancerous. So twice I have had to go back to his office to have "wide margins" removed. That means that he had to cut wide and deep around the area, to make sure that the entire thing was removed. I've had one lesion removed on my shoulder, and another removed on my foot.

If you don't have a dermatologist, ask your primary care physician about whether you should see one. The National Cancer Institute website notes that there are 76,000 new cases of melanoma diagnosed every year in the US, and over 10,000 people die from melanoma every year in the US. My dermatologist is trying to make sure that I'm not one of them.

At my most recent dermatologist appointment, I had two irregular looking moles removed. I had bandages, and I had to do a little bit of wound care. It was not a big deal. This is part of preventive health care.

• • •

Skin is a funny thing. I have it, I'm in it. It is sort of like a container for me, or of me. I wash it, I shampoo some of it, I shave some of it. I cover parts of it, especially when it's cold. I put sunscreen on some of it when it's hot and sunny outside. But I don't think about my skin much, except when I have a dermatologist appointment.

We have a lot of expressions about skin in our language. "Thin skinned" means someone who is sensitive, and "thick skinned" means someone who is not so sensitive. One expression that I use a lot is "comfortable in my own skin." I was trying to explain what this expression means to a friend from another country, and the best explanation I could think of was "at peace with myself."

My skin has a lot of moles and spots. It also has about 100 places that used to have moles, but the dermatologist took those away for safe keeping. My skin also has me inside of it. I'm learning to be at peace inside this container, for however long I get to keep the container.

★ ★ ★ ★ ★
When an Intruder Broke into My Home

"What was that?"

It was the middle of the night in February 1993. Theresa and I were sound asleep, and were woken suddenly by loud noises above us.

"What was that?"

At first it sounded like someone was walking on the roof. There was definitely movement above us. Footsteps.

The next sound that I heard will stay with me forever. That was the sound of our house being broken into.

• • •

I called 911 and explained the situation. Noises on the roof, and then sounds of a break-in. And now I can hear footsteps in the attic above us. The dispatcher sent a patrol car right away, and asked me to stay on the line.

Within a couple of minutes, the patrol car arrived, and the dispatcher connected the officer in the patrol car onto our call. He asked us to stay put while he analyzed the situation.

He was quiet for a minute or two, and then he started laughing. He said, "you can come outside now, it's okay."

• • •

When Theresa and I went outside, the officer was shining a flashlight near the roof of our house. Just beneath the roof, there was a set of metal eaves that had been broken, with a gaping hole in the front of the house where the eaves used to be.

In the middle of the hole, there was a raccoon throwing attic insulation out of the house.

After we regained our composure, we asked the police officer what to do about the raccoon. He suggested that we call an exterminator. In the morning, we called our exterminator, but they explained that raccoons were not something that they dealt with. We would have to call a wildlife company.

Later that day, we identified a wildlife company that would come out and assess the situation. They assessed the situation (and the size of our bank account, I think) and proposed a solution that would remove the raccoon, and our life savings, from the house.

Raccoons don't normally break into homes in the middle of the night. The wildlife expert explained that raccoons look for nesting areas in the wintertime, right before giving birth. The raccoon in our attic was probably a pregnant one, who may or may not have given birth in our attic.

Over the next few days, the wildlife company cleaned out our attic (Mom Raccoon had left and had not given birth yet). The raccoon did tear our attic up, so it had to be re-insulated. The wildlife company installed barriers so that Mom Raccoon couldn't return.

I never did get back to sleep that night . . .

* * * * *

Darwin Park

(I wrote this in 2015, right before I published my first book, Can Openers.)

There is an expression, "The joy is in the journey, not the destination." But I think about the destination a lot. Yogi Berra once said something like, "If you don't know where you're going, how will you know when you get there?"

I recently found a park near where I live. It is a destination.

I take Darwin there a couple of times a week. I call the place Darwin Park because Darwin has marked most of the park as his own.

I use walks in Darwin Park as meditation time. These are some of the things I think about when I walk around Darwin Park:

I think Pennsylvania is one of the prettiest places in the world, three seasons a year. We have the most beautiful springs, summers, and falls.

I hope that no one discovers Darwin Park.

• • •

I am starting to think about what life will be like as an "empty nester." My older daughter is a year away from graduating college, and my younger daughter may be three years from going away to school. There is something bittersweet about the thought of them moving out and moving on. On the one hand, they are growing into exactly who they should be. On the other hand, I will miss them once they leave.

Dinners at our house are like a contact sport. Sometimes I can't get a word in edgewise, and I love it.

• • •

My wedding anniversary is next weekend. (I think if I write about it now, maybe I will remember it on Sunday.) Twenty-three years ago,

I married my best friend. Twenty-three years later, she is still my best friend.

My best friend enjoys travel more than anyone else I know. She tolerates all of the indignities of travel (cramped airline seats, airsick children, time zone changes, fatigue) and makes every trip an adventure.

One more note about my best friend. Twice people have met me and said, "Your wife must be a saint." I'm not sure how I feel about that. Except that she is a saint. She is the most selfless person I've ever met. She sacrifices for her family and her friends in a way that I've never seen before.

• • •

One of my friends used to say, "The sign of real maturity is when you can be joyous about someone else's success, even when it comes at the expense of yourself." I'm working on that.

• • •

I think it is time to publish my book. Several people have recently asked me when I am going to publish it.

In order to publish it, I have to learn how to do a number of things I don't know how to do right now, like indexing, formatting, cover art, and obtaining copyright clearance. I think I will spend a lot of money publishing my book. I think my ego will take a hit when only three people purchase it.

• • •

Regardless of how many people purchase the book, I have thoroughly enjoyed writing it so far. I've enjoyed it so much that I'm starting to think of doing it as my fourth career.

I've had three careers so far. I spent my first years out of college working in a research lab. Then I went back to pharmacy school and spent several years as a dispensing pharmacist. Since 1994, I've worked in the pharmaceutical industry. I love what I do, and I have a great job.

My dream right now is to be able to do two careers at the same time: my career in the pharmaceutical industry, and my work as an author. The truth is that's exactly what I've been doing for the past year. I think about my day job, and I love it. I think about writing, and I love that, too.

In a time when fewer and fewer people are making a living at writing, I consider myself lucky to be able to write for fun and for friends. But there is a little part of me that would love to write a bestseller.

• • •

ARTS & ENTERTAINMENT

I love live entertainment. I have attended over 400 concerts, and count-less sporting events and shows. Here are some of my favorite essays about entertainment. I wrote this section in 2016.

★ ★ ★ ★ ★
When the House Lights Go Down

I love to see live sports and entertainment. One of my favorite things in the world is the buzz in the crowd right before the show or the game begins. The seats are full, the crowd is electric ... and then the house lights go down.

I love that feeling because at that moment, anything is possible. I don't know what the band is going to play, I don't know how the home team is going to do. I've seen a lot of concerts and sporting events. I've probably seen 400 concerts, and scores of Eagles, Phillies, Flyers and Sixers games (including playoff games for all four teams, and championship games for the Eagles and Flyers), as well as a number of college and high school events.

I've seen a lot of house lights go down.

• • •

T he best version of "when the house lights go down" is when there is an
extra something in the air. Something that makes the event a little bit
more special. Something that makes that show or game unique, or different, from all of the other shows happening that night. For example:

1. The first show of the tour: You never know what's going to happen
   on the first show of the tour. There are no setlists to check from
   previous shows, there are no concert reviews in yet. I've seen a lot
   of tour openers. These shows are often a little rough around the
   edges, but a lot of fun to see.

2. The last show of the tour: This type of show can be poignant. If the
   band has been on the road for two years, or it's a playoff game and
   the entire season comes down to this game, it can be emotional.

3. The big-publicity show or event: I've been to a Super Bowl, NFC
   Championship games, a Final Four, the Stanley Cup Finals, and
   Live Aid. You know it's a big event when there are satellite trucks
   outside, and blimps and helicopters flying overhead.

4. The exotic-venue show: Sometimes bands search for a special place
   to play a show. This is usually a small theater, or a beautiful out-
   door setting. I've seen concerts at Radio City Music Hall, Red Rocks
   Amphitheatre in Colorado, and the Greek Theater in Berkeley.
   All of them make a spectacular setting for a great evening of
   entertainment.

5. The smallest venue of the tour: Sometimes bands seek out a smaller
   venue for some of their shows, in search of some intimacy with
   their fans. I seek out these shows. If a band is playing 60,000-seat
   stadiums and offers a show in a 5,000-seat theater, I want to see
   the theater show. It's easier to attend, and I know that all of the
   fans who attend are there for the show. I once saw the reunited
   Little Feat in their first show back after Lowell George's death. They
   played (believe it or not) in a fast-food joint on Penn's campus. I
   also saw David Crosby (along with Graham Nash) play his first show
   after release from prison, at the Valley Forge Music Fair.

6. The album show: Some bands with large catalogs are now offering shows where they re-create an album from start to finish. I've seen the Who play *Tommy* and *Quadrophenia*, and Bruce Springsteen play *Born to Run*, *Born in the U.S.A.*, and *The River*.

7. The secret show: This is on my bucket list. Some bands do rehearsal shows before their tours begin. The Rolling Stones will play in a club, and Bruce Springsteen will play a show in a small theater, before their tours begin. I haven't been able to attend one of these yet, but I'm still trying . . .

* * * * *

Cutting the Cord

(I wrote this essay in 2016, about trying to cancel our cable package. It took me almost a year to do it.)

My family and I have had cable TV for as long as cable TV has been available. It is finally time to stop paying the cable company. We are cutting the cord.

For those of you who don't know, "cutting the cord" means cutting ties with cable/internet/TV providers. What was once a few people is not turning into a tide. Just this week, I have learned about three families I know who have either cut the cord or are actively trying to do so.

There are a lot of reasons for cutting the cord, and for us, the best reason is the money. We reviewed our cable bill and were shocked at how much we pay. It's not like I planned to spend this much money twenty years ago. It just seemed to happen.

We are paying $300 a month for cable, and we hardly watch any TV at all.

Goodbye cable.

• • •

The average American family watches about thirty-five hours of TV a week. I don't think that we watch thirty-five hours of TV a year. Really. The last TV shows that I watched were

part of the Eagles game on Monday night;

the Villanova–UNC college basketball final game;

the Super Bowl.

That's my TV watching so far in 2016. It's September. There is no need for me to pay for television anymore.

• • •

Okay, so maybe I am not ready to go cold turkey yet. I would like to watch a football game sometimes. Maybe I would like to watch the news if there is an evolving situation.

I have done a little bit of research, and with an antenna (no more rabbit ears, today's antennae are fancier than that) and a small box, I can receive about twenty channels, including CNN and ESPN, for about $20 a month and an initial $100 for antenna.

So my total annual cost should go from about $3600 to about $250. I like that.

• • •

What I really want for television is to be able to choose exactly which channels I want to watch, and when I want to watch them. If I want to watch a football game on TV, I am willing to pay five to ten dollars to do that. I watch ten to fifteen games a year.

That is all that I want.

But cable and internet providers don't want to provide me just that amount of TV. They want to sell me big packages of channels that I don't want to watch. I'm tired of paying for stuff that I don't watch.

So we've started the process of cutting the cord. I've identified some-one who knows how to install antennae and the box that provides a minimal channel package. I think we can finish this in the next couple of weeks.

I won't miss the big cable bills. I won't miss having 500 channels that I don't watch. I won't miss having cable equipment all over the place.

But I will miss the outstanding customer service that my cable company provides.

★ ★ ★ ★ ★

When Radio Was King

I grew up listening to radio in the 1960s and 1970s. When my parents were in the car, they sometimes listened to WIBG or WFIL. I remember listening to the Beatles for the first time while driving around in the car with my parents.

Radio stations and disc jockeys were very popular back then. One station, WIBG, had a group of disc jockeys called the "WIBG Good Guys." Bill Wright Sr., a friend of mine, was one of those disc jockeys. I have a photo of Bill during a press conference with the Beatles in 1964. At the time, the Beatles were the most popular celebrities in the world. Radio disc jockeys weren't far behind. At his peak of popularity in the 1960s, Bill had a 52 radio share. That means that 52% of the radios in Philadelphia were tuned into WIBG while Bill was on the air. Today the largest radio share will be during a snowstorm, and KYW will be lucky to get a share of 10.

• • •

I started listening to the radio in earnest in the mid-1970s. My friends introduced me to rock and roll. At the time, there were three popular FM rock and roll radio stations in Philadelphia: WMMR (93.3), WYSP (94.1), and WIOQ (102).

Disc jockeys at the time were stars and celebrities in the own right. A disc jockey could jump-start the career of an artist or a band. Music stars would stop in at radio stations when they were touring, in order to plug their latest album and their concert.

One well-known example of this was Ed Sciaky, a popular Philadelphia-area disc jockey, who introduced Philadelphia to the music of Bruce Springsteen. He played a lot of Bruce's first record on the radio and was responsible for Bruce's early popularity here. Bruce Springsteen mentioned Ed Sciaky by name in his recent autobiography as a major contributor to his early popularity.

• • •

I was a WMMR listener. I listened to "The Morning Zoo," a show that played from 6–10 a.m. and featured John DeBella and his sidekick Mark Drucker, aka Mark the Shark. (Mark has since passed away.) John DeBella is still on the air in Philadelphia, but now on WMGK.

The Morning Zoo was so popular that they broadcast live shows in the early 1980s. They rented halls and did their shows in front of a live audience. I attended two of them. Those live shows were so popular that I had to stand outside in a line in order to get into the hall.

The Morning Zoo used to do a daily feature called the Dreaded Morning Oldie, or "DMO" for short. John DeBella would play an isolated segment from a song (sometimes only a single note from the song), and listeners would call in and try to guess the song. The first listener to identify the song would win a prize. To this day, I play a version of this with my wife.

One of my favorite radio memories is that WIOQ used to occasionally offer a weekend-long promotion (Friday afternoon through Sunday evening) called "The Best of Progressive Rock." Once or twice a year, they would schedule the music for the entire weekend in advance, publish the schedule in the newspaper, and would block thirty or sixty minutes at a time for particular artists. For example, the Beatles might be on Saturday night from 10 to 11 p.m., and the Rolling Stones would be on from 11 p.m. to midnight. The most popular artists were played between 7 p.m.

and midnight on Friday and Saturday nights, and the least popular artists were played between 2 and 6 a.m.

• • •

Radio was a communal experience for my friends and me. I explain some of this to my daughters, and they look at me as if I have two heads. The idea that my friends and I would schedule our weekends around the play schedule of a radio station is something that they don't understand. They don't have "communal experiences" like that anymore.

My parents used to describe watching the most popular TV shows (*The Tonight Show Starring Johnny Carson*, or *The Milton Berle Show*) and talking about those shows with friends the next day. Philadelphia radio was the same for me. My friends and I shared that common bond.

I miss hearing "93.3, WMMR. The Home of Rock and Roll."

★ ★ ★ ★ ★
The Taping Pit

(I wrote this essay in 2017 after the publication of my first book, Can Openers: Essays on Life and Love. The book turned out to be a best seller. In other words, it was the best-selling book I ever published.)

The Grateful Dead played more than 2300 concerts, beginning in 1964. They took a different approach to making music and selling music than their contemporaries. Most other bands recorded albums and toured in order to support the album. The Grateful Dead toured, and occasionally recorded an album to meet contractual obligations.

They preferred playing live music for their fans rather than recording albums in the studio, because they enjoyed the relationship that they had with their fans. They started a mailing list in an effort to update their fans on what they were doing.

They allowed their fans to tape their concerts, which was revolutionary at the time. The fans who taped their concerts became known as "tapers," and eventually so many people wanted to tape their concerts that the Grateful Dead had to create a "taping pit," a section of each arena or stadium where tapers could set up their taping equipment.

Music industry executives and fans of other bands didn't understand taping. The first reaction was "You're giving away your music—that's a terrible idea." But the Grateful Dead understood their fans and their music, and realized that the best way to spread the word about their music was to give it away. "The shows are never the same, ever," Jerry Garcia once said. "When we're done with it, they can have it."

I first came to know and love the music of the Grateful Dead through some of these tapes. My first exposure to the Grateful Dead was listening to concerts on tape, not by listening to their albums.

• • •

My book *Can Openers* was released last week. I have had the following five experiences in the past five days:

1. Yesterday, I Googled my book and myself. I learned that someone in Australia is re-selling ten copies of my book for about thirty dollars apiece.
2. Someone else has taken my book and made a PDF version of it available for distribution.
3. My book made it into the top twenty in its category (humor essays) after five days on the market.
4. I walked into my exercise class this morning and one of my classmates congratulated me on my book release (I never told her about my book).
5. Someone that I don't know sent me an email this weekend, asking what the twenty-four-letter word was in my essay "Soft Shoulder."

When I started my website (halwardblog.com, now also halward.blog), my first essay was entitled "Is This Thing On?" The idea was that I was (metaphorically speaking) setting up a microphone and speaking into it for the first time. I created the blog for fun and for free. My hope was that I could write, and maybe people would read it.

I took a moment to look up from my microphone this weekend, and it looks like there are people in the taping pit.

* * * * *
Dear Basketball Gods

(I wrote this letter in April 2016, after Villanova won the basketball national championship. My daughter and I attended the Final Four in Houston. Go Cats!)

Dear Basketball Gods,   April 3-5, 2016

April 3, 2016: Thank you for letting Heather and I go to Houston to follow the improbable Villanova NCAA tournament run. It has been a lot of fun so far.

A few random thoughts about the Final Four experience:

Watching an NCAA Final Four is a weird experience. A Final Four means that four different teams are involved, and four different fan bases are there. Unlike a typical sporting event where there is a home team and an away team, every team at a Final Four is an away team. Each of the four teams had a few thousand fans in the stadium. But there were also Houston locals who wanted to be there for the experience, and some hardcore basketball fans who wanted to see the Final Four. The feeling in the stadium was different from a typical sporting event, in a way that is hard to explain.

Being at a Final Four involves watching a basketball game in a stadium. Our seats were upstairs, so the viewing was difficult.

Tickets for a Final Four are relatively inexpensive. By comparison, tickets to a Super Bowl are at least $5000 now, and tickets to a Final Four are available for $200–$250. Tickets to the final game drop to $50 or so, because fans of the losing semifinal teams leave town without attending the finals.

The game between Villanova and Oklahoma was weird. The final score (95–51) looked like a blowout. And it was a blowout. But it didn't feel like a blowout for much of the game.

At the half, Villanova was up by 14 points. In the first four minutes of the second half, Oklahoma played a pressing defense, and whittled the Villanova lead to 9 points. Villanova fans looked nervous. Over the next four minutes, both teams played sloppily. With twelve minutes left, I looked at the score, and Villanova was up by 15. I started telling Heather that I thought the game might be over . . .

What happened next was historic. Villanova went on a 25-0 run. Their defense appeared to overwhelm Oklahoma. I read online that had Villanova not scored a point in the first half, they still scored enough points in the second half alone to win the game.

• • •

I have mixed feelings about writing this blog. Heather and I are in the airport preparing to come home. Our plan is that Heather wants to be on campus to (hopefully) celebrate the national championship victory on Monday night.

But we really wanted to stay. We started pricing two additional nights at our hotel, and different air arrangements, and ... and finally we said, "Let's go home."

The truth is that we will see a lot more of the final game on television. Watching a basketball game in a stadium isn't easy.

But I want to stay.

• • •

Kudos to Nova Nation. You presented yourself really well this week. Every Villanova student, and every Villanova alum, was positive and friendly. Houston thinks highly of you.

I'm not a Villanova alum, and I'm not a Villanova student. I'm just a Nova dad. But I'm proud to be associated with Villanova. They are molding future leaders.

• • •

Kudos also to the city of Houston for a job well done. They absorbed the Final Four, and all of its March Madness, without blinking.

Houston is also scheduled to host the next Super Bowl, and also the next NBA All Star Game. Good for them. The city was pleasant, and modern, and we had a lot of fun for our brief visit.

If the Eagles go to the Super Bowl, I will gladly return.

• • •

Heather and I had a brief "perspective" experience on our ride back to the airport. Our driver was a fellow from Kenya. This gentleman grew up in a village with very little, by US standards. On most days, a once-daily meal was not a guarantee. He didn't wear a pair of shoes until he was seventeen.

He now works two jobs and goes to nursing school. His village sponsored the cost of his travel to the United States six years ago. Now he sends money back to his village and his family.

This man has a uniformly positive attitude about life in the United States. He loves living here, and he loves the opportunity that he has here. He noted that he no longer worries about whether he will have a meal each day.

I hopped into his car for our ride back to the airport, feeling sorry for myself about leaving Houston early. I finished the ride to the airport grateful for all that is right in my life.

Thank you, Basketball Gods.

• • •

April 5, 2016: I should note that I wrote all of that in between the semi-finals and the final game, which was played last night. Villanova won that game, 77-74.

If you're not a basketball fan, go watch a video of the last 4.7 seconds of the game. It was the best finish to a college basketball game that I've ever seen.

Congratulations to Villanova and all of its students. Nova Nation has a lot to be proud of today. They have a lot to be proud of every day.

And that is coming from a Penn and PCPS grad who is married to a St. Joseph's grad.

• • •

I attended Super Bowl XXXIX on February 6, 2005. The Eagles lost to the Patriots.

I returned to work on the Tuesday after the Super Bowl. One of my colleagues said to me, "I don't understand why you're disappointed—it's just a game!"

Maybe it is just a game. But people care about games. There is a reason that the most watched TV show every year is a game.

There is a reason that our stadiums and arenas fill up for football, baseball, basketball, and hockey.

There is a reason my daughter partied like it was 1985 last night on Villanova's campus.

There is a reason that I went to the Super Bowl, and that Heather and I went to the Final Four.

These games matter to me.

* * * * *

Drafting NFL Players Blindfolded

(I published this essay in 2016, during a dark time in Philadelphia Eagles history.)

On April 28, 2016, NFL Commissioner Roger Goodell will step to the microphone and state, "With the first pick in the 2016 NFL Draft, the Los Angeles Rams select ..." More people will watch that announcement than will watch the World Series, the NBA Championship or the NHL Stanley Cup Finals.

In other words, more people will watch a guy in a suit rip open an envelope than will watch the finals of any of the other major sports in the US

• • •

When the draft occurs, it is expected that the first two teams to draft (the Los Angeles Rams and the Philadelphia Eagles) will draft quarterbacks.

Both teams participated in big trades this week in order to move up in the draft. The Rams traded away six draft picks to move into the first draft slot, and the Eagles traded away five draft picks to move into the second slot.

These are the same teams that traded with each other for quarterbacks on March 13, 2015. The Eagles sent Nick Foles to the Rams, and the Rams sent Sam Bradford to the Eagles. That trade was so bad for both teams that they are each gambling away two years of draft picks for a brand-new quarterback this year.

• • •

What is really strange about the Eagles' plans this year is that they just signed two quarterbacks to very rich contracts. Sam Bradford and

Chase Daniel signed deals with over $25 million in guaranteed money. Why did the Eagles sign two quarterbacks to guaranteed contracts, and then trade away five draft picks in order to pick another quarterback?

It occurs to me that maybe the Philadelphia Eagles have no idea what they are doing.

But other teams also don't know what they're doing. I saw a list of teams who traded up in order to draft a quarterback in the top five in the last twenty-five years. The quarterbacks who were selected are Robert Griffin III, Mark Sanchez, Michael Vick, Ryan Leaf, Kerry Collins and Jeff George.

That is an atrocious group of quarterbacks.

• • •

The NFL commissioner will not tell you a few things next week:

The majority of the players drafted next weekend won't be playing football in four years. The average career length in the NFL is now 3.2 years.

Most of the players who are drafted don't work out. Teams have no idea what they are getting when they draft a player. You don't believe me? Search for the draft picks your favorite team made the past three years. I just did that for the Eagles draft picks from 2014–2016. In that time they had twenty-one draft picks. I think six of those players are still with the team. One or two have made substantial contributions.

The NFL and its teams spend a fortune on the NFL draft process. They would be better off by putting on blindfolds and throwing darts at a dartboard. Their chances of draft success would be the same, and they would save themselves a lot of money.

* * * * *

The Sugar Magnolia Rule

(I wrote this essay in 2017 about a twenty-year streak of bad sports/concert luck that I had been having. At the end of the essay, I wrote "Maybe the Eagles will win the Super Bowl this year." If you don't believe me, go read the original post, on HalWardBlog.com. By the way—the Eagles did win it, on February 4, 2018. More about that later ...)

The Grateful Dead album *American Beauty* was released in 1970. The album included ten songs, including concert staples like "Truckin'," "Box of Rain," "Friend of the Devil," and the third song, "Sugar Magnolia."

The album version of "Sugar Magnolia" is okay, but nothing special. It lasts three minutes and nineteen seconds, and has a nice groove. But in concert, the Grateful Dead transformed it into an epic show closer. Every third or fourth show, they would end a show with it, with fans dancing in the aisles for every second of the ten to fifteen minutes that the Dead played it. (The Grateful Dead played a different setlist every night, so this song, and every song, was only played when they felt like playing it.)

"Sugar Magnolia" is my favorite song. Theresa and I were at a number of shows in the '80s and early '90s where it was played, including one New Year's concert where the Grateful Dead brought in the new year (1989) with an epic version, with Clarence Clemons guesting on saxophone.

But sometime around 1992, something unfortunate happened. I stopped seeing "Sugar Magnolia" in concert. It was strange. The Dead would play it either the show before a show that I attended, or at the show after a show I attended. But not at the show I attended.

My friends Alan and Rich started noticing a pattern. They called it "the Sugar Magnolia Rule." If I was at a show, the Grateful Dead were not going to play "Sugar Magnolia."

This has gone on now for twenty-three years. No kidding. If Alan and Rich attend a show without me, the band plays "Sugar Magnolia." If I'm there, no chance.

• • •

The Sugar Magnolia Rule meant that I was unlucky. And my bad luck wasn't limited to the Grateful Dead. It extended to other concerts. Theresa, Alan, and I left a U2 concert early. (It was hot, it was very crowded, and we weren't having a very good time.) The next day, we learned that Bruce Springsteen joined U2 for the encore.

An encore that we missed.

• • •

The Sugar Magnolia Rule started extending into the sports world, too. If I attended a sporting event, bad things happened.

I attended Super Bowl XXXIX. The Eagles were tied with the Patriots after three quarters. They lost the game 24–21.

Theresa and I attended a National League Championship Series deciding game, and watched as the Phillies were knocked out of the playoffs.

I watched the Edmonton Oilers knock the Flyers out of the Stanley Cup finals.

And last year, I attended the NCAA semifinals. Villanova won that game. Heather and I debated about whether to stay or not. We came home for the finals. Since I wasn't there, Villanova won.

• • •

On Saturday night, I attended a concert (Phil Lesh and Friends), and after a gap of about 8,395 days, I saw a "Sugar Magnolia."

The Curse of the Bambino is over.

Maybe the Eagles will win the Super Bowl this year.

* * * * *

Waiting for the Playoffs

(I am a lifelong Philadelphia-area resident. I wrote this in 2017, during a dark period in Philadelphia sports history.)

The Philadelphia Phillies were last in the playoffs in 2011. That year, they lost in the National League Divisional Series. That was six years ago.

The Philadelphia Flyers were last in the playoffs in 2016. They lost in the first round. Before that, they were in the playoffs in 2014, when they lost in the first round. They last won a playoff round in 2011. That was six years ago.

The Philadelphia Sixers were last in the playoffs in 2012. They lost in the second round. That was five years ago.

The Philadelphia Eagles lost their first game in the playoffs in 2013, 2012, and 2009. They last won a playoff game in 2008. That was nine years ago.

• • •

The Flyers did not make the playoffs this year.
The Sixers did not make the playoffs this year.
The Phillies have the worst record in baseball right now (twenty-nine teams have a better record than they do today). They will not make the playoffs this year.
And the Philadelphia Eagles may be the worst team in their division.
Darwin and I are looking for a playoff team in Philadelphia. I think it's going to be a long wait.

* * * * *

Roman Numerals

(I wrote this essay late November 2017, when I thought that the Eagles might go to the playoffs. Then on December 12, 2017, Carson Wentz—the Philadelphia Eagles quarterback—tore his ACL. As far as I was concerned, the Eagles season was finished. Little did I know ...)

• • •

I am a lifelong fan of the Philadelphia Eagles. "Lifelong," as in I have been attending Philadelphia Eagles games since my father took me to Franklin Field when I was four years old. I've seen games at Franklin Field, Veterans Stadium (section 722, where I learned how to speak Philadelphian), the Linc, and a few games on the road, too.

A Philadelphia Eagles fan who claims to be a lifelong fan is also a long-suffering fan. The Eagles have never won a Super Bowl. The last championship that they won was on December 26, 1960, before there was such a thing as a Super Bowl.

That 1960 championship happened 368 days before I was born.

• • •

If you watch any professional football, you know that the Eagles have the best record right now. They have a 9-1 record, and the next closest team in their own division is the Dallas Cowboys at 5-5.

Their one loss, to the Kansas City Chiefs, happened back in September. If the Eagles played the Chiefs today, the Eagles would win by twenty points. The last time the Eagles won by less than ten points was five weeks ago.

• • •

In the interest of total honesty, before the season started, I looked at the schedule, and I made a prediction about the Eagles season. I predicted that they would go 9-7. They are 9-1 right now. Unless the wheels fall off of this team, I underpredicted. I wrote an essay in June called "Waiting for the Playoffs." I didn't think this team would make the playoffs this year.

This was a team with big problems in the backfield (cornerback and safety), and question marks about the passing game. I never imagined that they would fix the backfield mess, have the best running defense in the NFL, improve the passing game, and have a respectable rushing offense, too.

This is a team that lost their left tackle (Jason Peters), running back (Darren Sproles), and a linebacker (Jordan Hicks). They've done without a star cornerback (Ronald Darby) for eight weeks. They even played half of their last game without a field goal kicker, and did just fine without him.

All of this success hinges on one person: Carson Wentz. Playing in only his second year, I did not think he would be this good, this fast. He has very good presence of mind. He sees things on the football field that others do not, and he is able to make throws that few other quarterbacks can. In addition, when his protection falls apart, he can scramble and pick up a first down, which is a nice thing to be able to do.

This is my highest praise for a quarterback: I cannot remember the last time he made a decision and I thought, "Why did he DO that?!" He is playing mistake-free football right now.

Football Gods, please keep Carson Wentz healthy.

• • •

I attended Super Bowl XXXIX on February 6, 2005 in Jacksonville, between the Philadelphia Eagles and The New England Patriots. The Eagles lost that game 24-21. The game was tied at the end of the third quarter, 14-14. The Eagles had a chance.

Unfortunately, my team was coached by a fellow who didn't understand how to save timeouts or run a two-minute drill, and my quarterback threw up on the field when things got tense. The other team had Bill Belichick as coach and Tom Brady at quarterback, so there were no rings for Philadelphia that day.

As I was leaving my seat that day, a kind New England Patriots fan sitting near me stopped me. He saw how upset I was, and he said "Don't worry; your team is great. You'll be back."

He didn't understand what "long suffering" means.

$$\bullet \ \bullet \ \bullet$$

Enough about suffering. The Eagles team this year is good. Really good. Good enough that I'm starting to look at Super Bowl LII tickets in sunny Minneapolis, Minnesota. (What kind of sunscreen do I need in Minneapolis in February?)

I know that is premature. But the idea that the Eagles are good is such a strange idea that I don't know what to do with it. If the Boston Red Sox, Chicago Cubs, and the City of Cleveland can end their streaks, why not the Philadelphia Eagles?

★ ★ ★ ★ ★

Postscript

(I wrote this on December 12, 2017):

The answer to "why not the Philadelphia Eagles" is "Carson Wentz's ACL."

* * * * *

Fly Eagles Fly

(I wrote this essay just prior to the Eagles playing in Super Bowl LII, on February 4, 2018. I attended the game with my cousin Howard.)

The Philadelphia Eagles are going to Super Bowl LII, to be played next Sunday, February 4, 2018, in sunny Minneapolis, Minnesota. This is only their third trip to the Super Bowl. They lost to the Oakland Raiders in Super Bowl XV, and lost to the New England Patriots in Super Bowl XXXIX.

I was eighteen years old for Super Bowl XV. I painted my face green for the game, which I watched with my roommate in our dorm room. It was a decision I regretted, as the Eagles didn't play very well that day. They lost 27–10, but the game wasn't even that close.

I was forty-three for Super Bowl XXXIX. Instead of painting my face green, I went to the Super Bowl in Jacksonville. That Super Bowl was much closer (the game was tied after three quarters), but my team had a coach who had clock-management issues and a quarterback with regurgitation issues, and the Eagles lost 24–21.

I'm fifty-six years old now, and the Eagles are going to the Super Bowl again. So I have to go to the Super Bowl again. That is how it is. I have been going to Eagles games since I was four years old, when the Eagles played their games on a college campus (Franklin Field).

• • •

In the movie *Tangled* (a remake of the Rapunzel tale), Rapunzel is talking to her friend about her dream of looking at the night sky. She says, "I've been looking out of a window for eighteen years, dreaming about what I might feel like when those lights rise in the sky. What if it's not everything I dreamed it would be?"

Her friend says, "It will be."

Rapunzel then asks "And what if it is? What do I do then?"

Her friend replies, "Well, that's the good part I guess. You get to go find a new dream."

Watching the Philadelphia Eagles win the Super Bowl would be a dream come true for me. Celebrating a Super Bowl victory is on my bucket list. I want to check that off my list next week.

• • •

The 2004 Boston Red Sox won a World Series for the first time in their team history. That win meant a lot to so many people in the Boston area. Sportswriter Bill Simmons wrote a book called *Now I Can Die in Peace* about that season and that World Series victory.

In the book, he wrote about generations of families who celebrated the victory together, and about offerings made at cemeteries, churches, and temples to honor the victory.

My father took me to all of the Eagles games I attended in the 1960s and 1970s. I will bring him a souvenir from the Super Bowl. (I offered to take him, but he isn't up for the travel anymore.)

My mother, who died in 2009, had a treasured Eagles blanket at her nursing home. When she died, I took that blanket as a treasured memory. I still have that blanket.

If the Eagles win next weekend, I am going to stop by her cemetery and let my mom know that they won. Then I'm going to visit my father and shake off fifty-six years of losing.

• • •

I would be willing to trade every Phillies World Series victory (two), every Flyers Stanley Cup (two), every Sixers World Championship (two), and every Villanova NCAA basketball championship, for one Super Bowl victory.

I'll even toss in Smarty Jones and Joe Frazier into the mix.

Just once is all that I ask.

Then I can die in peace.

* * * * *

My Super Bowl LII Diary

(I wrote this essay just after the Eagles won Super Bowl LII, on February 4, 2018. I attended the game with my cousin. "Watch the Eagles win a Super Bowl" was on my bucket list. I never thought I would have the experience.)

Satan walks into a hardware store and asks where he can purchase a snow shovel. The clerk looks at him and asks why he needs a snow shovel. Satan replies "Didn't you hear? The Philadelphia Eagles won the Super Bowl. Hell has frozen over!"

I just typed the words "the Philadelphia Eagles won the Super Bowl." I never thought that I would write those seven words.

• • •

In September of 2008, the Philadelphia Phillies started to falter. They had been in first place for much of the summer, but as the weather cooled, so did the Phillies. On September 10, they lost the third game (and the series) to the Florida Marlins, and fell three-and-a-half games behind the division-leading New York Mets. With only sixteen games to go in the season, I recall saying to Theresa, "The Phillies are done." At that point, they had a record of 79–67 (.541) and showed no signs of playoff hope.

I am a bad predictor. The next day, the Phillies went on a tear, winning seven in a row, and thirteen of their final sixteen games to win the National League East. They then won the Division Series 3–1 against Milwaukee, the National League Championship Series 4–1 against the LA Dodgers, and won the World Series 4–1 against Tampa Bay. After playing .541 baseball through one hundred forty-six games, they played .800 baseball for the final thirty games.

• • •

The reason that I mention "the Phillies are done" from ten years ago is that I recently said, "The Eagles are done." Carson Wentz tore his ACL and MCL in a game on December 10, 2017 against the LA Rams. The Eagles won the game, and were 11-2 after that win. But without Carson Wentz, I figured that the Eagles had no chance in the playoffs with Nick Foles.

I wasn't alone in that opinion. Las Vegas oddsmakers had the Eagles as 4-1 picks to win the Super Bowl before the Carson Wentz injury, and 14-1 picks to win after his injury.

Carson Wentz wasn't the only important member of the Philadelphia Eagles to suffer a season-ending injury this year. Jason Peters (left tackle), Jordan Hicks (linebacker), Darren Sproles (running back), Chris Maragos (safety and special teams) and Caleb Sturgis (kicker) all suffered season-ending injuries. Ronald Darby (cornerback) experienced an ankle injury in game one that kept him out for ten games.

Try winning a football game without your starting quarterback, left tackle, running back, linebacker, safety, cornerback and kicker. Go ahead, I'm waiting.

• • •

After Carson Wentz's injury, the Eagles finished the season by winning two of their last three games, although not very convincingly. Their regular season record was 13-3, but my hopes were not very high for play-off success.

After a bye week, they played the Atlanta Falcons and won 15-10, but only after Julio Jones (Atlanta Falcons) allowed a pass to go through his hands that would have won the game for the Falcons.

The following week, I attended the NFC Championship game against the Minnesota Vikings. The Vikings scored the opening touchdown, and took a 7-0 lead. They gained yardage on every play of their opening drive. I thought "uh-oh ..."

The Vikings never scored again. The Eagles won 37–7, and it didn't seem that close.

• • •

After the NFC Championship game, my cousin and I ordered a pair of tickets for Super Bowl LII in Minnesota. My feeling about the Super Bowl was, "If the Eagles are going, I am going."

So we went to the Super Bowl.

• • •

This Super Bowl was epic. The two teams set a number of records, including total yardage by a team (Patriots), total yardage by both teams combined, most points by the losing team (Patriots), fewest punts in a game, and most first downs passing by both teams.

There was a lot of offense in this game. The two teams combined for 1151 yards of total offense, and 874 yards of passing offense. The two teams set the record for most combined yardage in a Super Bowl by the end of the third quarter!

I saw something on the internet after the game, which noted that Tom Brady had 503 yards passing, 3 passing touchdowns, no interceptions, the Patriots had only 1 penalty for 5 yards, and never had to punt.

And they lost! How does a team throw for 503 yards, and lose?

• • •

I kept wondering, "How did the Eagles win a game in which the Patriots gained more yards (613 to 538), had more possessions (11 to 10), had less penalties and penalty yardage assessed, the same number of turnovers (1 apiece), and the Patriots never punted the ball?"

I looked at the drive charts. The Eagles and Patriots each had five drives in the first half. The Eagles scored on four of those drives (field goal, touchdown [with a missed extra point], touchdown [with missed two-point conversion], and touchdown) versus three Patriots scores (field goal, field goal, and touchdown [with a missed extra point]). In the second half, the Patriots had five drives, the Eagles had four. The Patriots scored on three drives (touchdown, touchdown, touchdown) and the Eagles scored on all four drives (touchdown, field goal, touchdown, field goal). The Eagles did not score on drives that ended in a punt and an interception. The Patriots did not score on drives that ended in a missed field goal, downs, the end of first half, a fumble, and the end of the game.

The Eagles scored on eight of their ten drives! The Patriots scored on six of their eleven drives.

The game was always close (at least it felt that way to me). The score was within ten points or less for all but one minute and twenty-four seconds. And the Patriots only led for seven minutes and one second. But that seven minutes and one second was in the heart of the fourth quarter, so it felt longer than that.

• • •

The Eagles were remarkably efficient when they had the ball. Almost historically so. They scored on 80% of their possessions! I did not realize that until I looked at the data.

• • •

None of this conveys the emotion of going to the Super Bowl and watching the Eagles win. Maybe a couple of stories will help.

After the game, I crossed the following item off of my bucket list, while I was still in the stadium: "Watch the Philadelphia Eagles win a Super Bowl." Done. Checked off. Complete.

• • •

I want to take a moment to thank all of the people in my life who have supported my Philadelphia Eagles habit. Let me start with my father, who started taking me to Eagles games when I was about four years old. Thank you also to Theresa, Heather and Dylan, who never complained about the time or the cost, because they know how happy I am watching the Philadelphia Eagles win. Thank you to my cousin Howard, who went to the Super Bowl with me, and who sang and laughed and cried with me.

And lastly, I have a few apologies to make. I was wrong about several people, and I want to admit that publicly. I was wrong about the hiring of Doug Pederson, the coach of the Philadelphia Eagles. I thought that he would be an Andy Reid clone, and I am tired of Andy Reid. I was wrong about Howie Roseman, the General Manager of the Eagles. He constructed an incredible team, including Carson Wentz and Nick Foles. I was wrong about Carson Wentz and Nick Foles. I did not think they could win on a big stage like the Super Bowl. I was wrong about Jeff Lurie, too. I doubted whether he really wanted to do whatever it takes to put a winning football team on the field. When I saw the expression on his face when he accepted the Vince Lombardi trophy, I saw someone who was (almost) as happy as I was.

I thought it might be appropriate to finish this story with the lyrics to one of the most beautiful songs I've ever had the pleasure of singing with 70,000 of my closest friends:

Fly Eagles Fly!
On the road to victory,
Fight Eagles Fight!
Score a touchdown one, two, three!

Hit 'em low,
Hit 'em high,
And watch our Eagles fly!
Fly Eagles Fly!
On the road to victory!
E-A-G-L-E-S!
EAGLES!

* * * * *
Concerts Then and Now

I've attended a lot of rock concerts. My first concert was on June 11, 1977 at JFK Stadium in Philadelphia, with 100,000 of my closest friends. Concerts have changed a lot over the years.

Back in the day, concerts were announced on WMMR (93.3) or WYSP (94.1). I'd listen to John DeBella and Pierre Robert. Both are still broadcasting, by the way. Concert tickets were usually $5.50, $4.50 and $3.50, depending on the seat location.

In 1977, I purchased concert tickets at Ticketron. I did this by standing in line, in advance of the on-sale time, and I waited. I usually did this in a Wanamaker's, or a Gimbels, or a Lit Brothers store. That's where Ticketrons were located. The Ticketron operator (hopefully) was savvy enough to pull a lot of tickets all at once, so that we (the people in line) received the best tickets.

If a concert sold out, I was usually out of luck. I didn't want to go to a concert and deal with scalpers, so I missed a few that I really wanted to attend.

On the day of the concert, I'd drive up to the venue and pay a couple of dollars for parking. I'd attend the concert, leave, and that was it. I'd tell my friends the next day about it, and I'd wear my concert tour T-shirt.

• • •

Now I learn about concerts on the internet, months in advance. Tickets go on sale in waves, first to exclusive groups (fan club members, certain exclusive credit card holders, and VIPs). Tickets then go on sale to the general public.

Tickets are often at least $100, and may cost as much as $1000 for some "concert experiences," where you can meet the band, get some souvenirs, and sit in a great location. Tickets then become available on other websites, like StubHub. While concerts still sell out, if I want to go to a concert, it is always possible to go, if I'm willing to pay the price.

I can prepay for parking at some venues (although Philadelphia doesn't have this yet).

I usually know what the band will play, because I can follow the tour set lists on Setlist.fm. Try it sometime; I like the website a lot. If there is a band that you like, their setlists are probably posted there.

For some bands, I can purchase a copy of the concert (audio and/or video) in advance of the show, and take it home with me as a souvenir.

And if I'm interested, I can watch video of other shows the band has performed on YouTube, and (this is cool) there is an app called Periscope. If the band is performing right now, someone may be broadcasting it live on their smartphone. Try Periscope—it's a cool concept that is just catching on.

★ ★ ★ ★ ★
My Favorite Albums and Concerts

My Top 15 Album List

 The Beatles : *Abbey Road*

Pink Floyd : *Dark Side of the Moon*

The Rolling Stones: *Sticky Fingers*

The Who : *Tommy*

Led Zeppelin: *IV* (also known as *Zofo*)

Queen: *A Night at the Opera*

Lynyrd Skynyrd: *One More From the Road*

Fleetwood Mac: *Rumours*

The Eagles : *Hotel California*

Bruce Springsteen: *Born to Run*

Peter Frampton: *Frampton Comes Alive*

Eric Clapton: *Slowhand*

Dire Straits: *Brothers in Arms*
Grateful Dead: *American Beauty*
The Band: *The Last Waltz*

I have a few words of color commentary about these albums. One is that every album occurred midway through the artists' careers, or later. There are no albums on this list that were the first albums for the artists. In most cases, these albums were the fourth, fifth, or sixth album in their respective careers.

Another note is that I could easily have chosen the next (or the previous) album for many of these artists, without blinking an eye. I could have chosen The Who's *Quadrophenia*, or Pink Floyd's *Wish You Were Here*, or Bruce Springsteen's *Darkness on the Edge of Town*. These artists all have multiple great albums that were recorded in the same time period.

Of the fifteen albums, ten are by British bands (if you count Fleetwood Mac as British). The only US-based artists on the list are the Eagles, Bruce Springsteen, Lynyrd Skynyrd, the Band, and the Grateful Dead.

All were recorded in the time period of 1974–1978, except for the Beatles and the Stones.

I have seen every artist on this list in concert, except for the Beatles. In that case, I've seen Paul McCartney and Ringo Starr.

★ ★ ★ ★ ★

And Now, for My Top 10 Concert List (in chronological order)

(This was originally published March 30, 2015 at halwardblog.com.)

Peter Frampton, Lynyrd Skynyrd, Dickie Betts, and the J. Geils Band: JFK Stadium, June 11, 1977. My first concert. 100,000 people packed into JFK Stadium on a beautiful summer evening.

Ian Hunter: Central Park West, July 11, 1980. Ian Hunter was the lead singer and force behind Mott the Hoople. This concert was so good, he later wrote a song about it.

The Grateful Dead: Radio City Music Hall, October 25, 1980. The Grateful Dead did a run of shows at Radio City Music Hall in the fall of 1980. At each show, they performed three sets (one acoustic, and then two electric). I was lucky to get a ticket for this show, because tickets were hard to find.

Simon and Garfunkel: Central Park, September 19, 1981. This was the reunion concert for Simon and Garfunkel, who had not toured together in over a decade. 500,000 people turned out for this. I was one of them.

Live Aid: JFK Stadium, July 13, 1985. This is the granddaddy of them all. A concert full of reunions (Led Zeppelin, Crosby Stills Nash & Young, Black Sabbath), superstars (Bob Dylan, Eric Clapton, members of the Rolling Stones), and a live worldwide TV audience. The best concert I ever attended.

David Crosby and Graham Nash: Valley Forge Music Fair, November 28, 1986. The smallest venue on the list. This is a personal favorite. David Crosby had just been released from a Texas prison, and had not played live in a few years. Newly sober, he was itching to play in front of an audience. On the morning of the show, Crosby and Nash appeared on a local radio station, and the DJ (Pierre Robert) asked them to play a song at the concert ("Cowboy of Dreams"). Crosby explained that they had never played it live, and it would take practice to do so. The DJ had guitars in the studio, and told them that they could practice the song on his radio show. They practiced it on the radio, and then played it live for the first time that night to a rapturous audience.

Human Rights Now! (Amnesty International): JFK Stadium, September 19, 1988. This was another great show. Bruce Springsteen & the E Street Band, Peter Gabriel, Sting, Tracy Chapman and Youssou N'Dour

The Grateful Dead: Oakland Coliseum, December 31, 1988. For fans of the Grateful Dead, a New Year's show was the favorite show of the year.

This was no exception. Clarence Clemons (of the E Street Band) joined the Dead onstage for several songs. At midnight, Bill Graham (the concert promoter) rode across the Coliseum on a giant ball. Fireworks and balloons dropped, and Theresa and I danced in the New Year to "Sugar Magnolia." Find the video clip on YouTube.

The Rolling Stones: Newark, New Jersey, December 15, 2012. Bruce Springsteen, Lady Gaga, and others joined the Rolling Stones in this reunion show. It was shown worldwide as a pay-per-view event.

The Grateful Dead: Chicago, Illinois, July 3–5, 2015. If you're reading this far, you'll notice that (at the time I wrote this) this show hasn't happened yet. I'm going to the final shows of the Grateful Dead this summer. This one is a retirement party.

Honorable Mention: The Grateful Dead: Red Rocks Amphitheatre, Colorado, June 12–14, 1984, and Greek Theatre, Berkeley, California, June 14–16, 1985.

* * * * *

Music on the Bones

Imagine listening to your favorite music on an x-ray.

I was speaking to someone who was born in the USSR. We were discussing x-rays, and he noted that x-rays used to be used as record albums there. I asked him for an explanation, and this is what he told me.

Record albums were banned there for many years, as a way of controlling public opinion. Someone figured out a way to copy music onto x-rays, instead of copying it onto vinyl.

Your homework assignment is to go do an online search on the phrase "music on the bones." Check out the images. You'll see music albums copied onto old x-rays.

I don't know why, but that fascinates me.

* * * * *

The Advertising Illusion

When I first started my blog page, I noted (at least temporarily) that my page would be free of advertising. There were a couple of reasons for that. The first reason was that I felt that advertising was unnecessary for my page, and it would take away from what I was trying to achieve. The second reason was that it did not seem worth the time and effort to make just a few dollars a month.

My decision hasn't changed. The time and the effort to make just a few dollars a month still isn't worth it.

What has changed in the past couple of years is how intrusive advertising has become. In the two years since I started my blog, most of the traditional billboards on my drive to work have been converted to digital billboards. Because the advertisements change every ten seconds or so, I think I am more likely to look at them. So are you.

Taxi cabs now have seat-back TVs that can't be turned off or avoided. So do airplanes and airport baggage carousels. And both taxi and airport TVs play a lot of advertising.

The supermarket is full of unavoidable advertisements. The ads are on the floor, the overhead speaker, and on all of the shelves.

• • •

I thought that advertisers knew all of the ways to intrude into my peace and quiet, but recently I experienced a new low. I saw a box truck ahead of me on the turnpike that appeared to be glowing from a distance. This truck was driving about one to two blocks ahead of me. As I drove closer to it, I saw that the back of the truck and both sides of the truck were actually digital displays that were playing advertisements while the truck was moving. The effect was hypnotic—I did not want to look, but I couldn't help myself.

What will advertisers NOT do in order to advertise their products?

THINKING OUT LOUD,
PART III

The Luckiest Guy I Know

When Lou Gehrig retired in 1939, he made a speech that included the following words: "Fans, for the past two weeks you have been reading about a bad break I got. Yet today I consider myself the luckiest man on the face of the earth." Watch the speech online. It is one of the most powerful speeches of all time.

• • •

Lou Gehrig was diagnosed with amyotrophic lateral sclerosis (ALS), also now known as Lou Gehrig's Disease. He had a terminal diagnosis, and he knew it. Yet he considered himself the luckiest man on the face of the earth.

I want what Lou Gehrig had. Not ALS. I want the perspective that he had, to be able to feel like the luckiest man on the face of the earth despite his circumstances.

I sometimes refer to myself as "the luckiest guy I know." I borrowed the idea from Lou Gehrig. I figure he wouldn't mind. But I also sometimes add "but I forget that sometimes." In other words, I may be the luckiest guy I know, but I keep forgetting that.

• • •

A few years ago, one of my friends suggested that I read a book entitled *The Progress Paradox* by Gregg Easterbrook. The subtitle of the book explained the book's purpose: *How Life Gets Better While People Feel Worse.* The first half of the book explains the author's view that life is getting better. The second half of the book explains the author's view that people feel worse about life, even though it keeps getting better.

The author suggests very strongly that we all have access to things that didn't even exist one hundred years ago. Things like longer life spans and improved healthcare, , transportation, education, diet, exercise, and more. He suggests that even the poorest people in our society have access to things that didn't exist for royalty two hundred years ago.

I don't appreciate those things most of the time. I don't walk around every day remembering to be grateful for clean water, fresh air, sunshine, healthy food, transportation, and employment. I forget to be grateful most of the time.

Anyone who knows me well knows how lucky I am. I have been the recipient of incredible life advantages from family and friends and colleagues. I have role models and mentors who have guided me all the way to where I am today.

• • •

Like *The Progress Paradox*, my life is a paradox. I might be the luckiest person I know, but I keep forgetting it.

★ ★ ★ ★ ★
Lead Us Not into Temptation

My family and I watched the movie *Fences* this weekend. The movie is about a 1950s family, starring Denzel Washington and Viola Davis.

(Spoiler alert: I'm going to discuss some plot details here.) In the movie, the Denzel Washington character starts the movie with (what seems like) a small thread of a bad habit. He flirts with someone who isn't his wife. That habit evolves into a cancer that eats into the fabric of his family. By the end of the movie, he has fathered a child born out of wedlock and destroyed two families. My daughter described him as an Awful Human Being.

· · ·

The Lord's Prayer (Matthew 6: 9–13) includes the phrase "lead us not into temptation, but deliver us from evil." My sense is that temptation is a universal problem.

I say that not as a paragon of virtue, but as a fellow who has a temptation problem. I'll share one (sort of) socially acceptable example. I was kidnapped a few years ago by a family of vegetarians. They love being vegetarians and never discuss eating meat. It isn't an option for them. It still seems to be an option for me.

Sometimes I take my dog for a walk, and I smell the smell of my neighbors using their grills. I can smell that smell from one hundred yards away, if the wind is blowing in the right direction. When I smell that smell, my dog and I start talking about hopping over the fence and executing the Great Cheeseburger Caper. I'm drooling as I write that sentence.

Please lead me not into temptation. I can't afford the bail money.

· · ·

I know some people with temptation issues. This month, several of them seem to have issues with gambling. I have learned about people who have gambled away everything. By "everything," I do mean everything—houses, cars, careers, families. Everything.

I know a fellow who tells about coming back from a casino and not having the money to pay the toll to cross the bridge into Philadelphia. He gambled away everything that he had, until he had nothing left. Not even toll money. He hasn't gambled since.

I was in a casino in 1988, before a Rolling Stones concert in Atlantic City. I put a quarter in a slot machine, and a bucket full of quarters poured out. I won fifty dollars, back when fifty dollars seemed like a lot of money to me. I couldn't put those quarters back into the slot machine fast enough. Five minutes later, the money was all gone. I haven't been in a casino since.

• • •

The New Testament isn't the only part of the Bible that talks about temptation. The topic is discussed in the second verse of the Old Testament (Genesis 1: 2). Something about an apple. The instructions were very clear: Do Not Eat The Apple!

As I recall, Adam and Eve had a temptation problem too.

Temptation was also a theme in Greek mythology. The sirens were beings who tempted sailors toward a set of rocks. If the sailors listened to the song of the sirens, they steered their ships into the rocks and died. In order to avoid the sirens, sailors (it was said) had to be strapped to the masts to avoid their overwhelming temptation.

• • •

As I mentioned earlier, in 2016, I wrote an essay called "Role Models." It's in my book *Can Openers*. I think it is one of my best essays.

When I was young, my role models were rock stars and professional athletes. They had a lot of money, and (what looked like) very exciting lives. Then I noticed that my role models weren't living very long, or very happy, lives. So I changed my role models.

My current role models are very good at avoiding temptation. I don't know how they do it, exactly. But they are faithful to all of their responsibilities and commitments. They honor their wedding vows, and they show up to work every day. That faithfulness to their commitments looks really appetizing today. Even more appetizing than the cheeseburger smell from my neighbor's yard.

Please lead me not into temptation.

* * * * *

Opiates and Pain

(I wrote this essay in 2016. It is still true in 2019.)

Sometimes I make a sound when I'm surprised, that sounds like "huh."

I passed a billboard on the Pennsylvania Turnpike this morning. "152 Montgomery County residents died of drug overdoses in 2015."

I made a sound of "huh."

• • •

According to the Center for Disease Control's annual report, more Americans died of drug overdoses in 2015 than from car accidents. And a lot of Americans died in car accidents last year.

While I didn't know any of the 152 people who overdosed and died last year in Montgomery County, I know several people who have died as a result of overdoses in Chester County, and in Philadelphia County.

Pharmacists. Professional people. Family people. People like you and me.

• • •

Opiates are a class of pain medication that includes morphine, codeine, oxycodone, hydrocodone, and others. Some are available by prescription, and some (like heroin) are available illegally. They are very effective, and very potent, relievers of physical pain.

If I remember my pharmacy school classes well (there is no guarantee of that ...), opiates bind at the mu receptor in the central nervous system to create the effect of analgesia. In other words, they block pain by interacting at a cellular level. The effect can be so pleasurable that some users want to re-create the experience over and over again.

Opiates can be very addictive.

• • •

I just finished reading an article about an epidemic of fentanyl use in Canada. According to the article, fentanyl (an opiate one hundred times more potent than morphine) is widely available and can be ordered online. It is being mass-produced overseas and shipped directly to the homes of Canadian addicts.

In the United States, we have the same problem with oxycodone. American users purchase prescription opiates online (or on the street, or with a physician's prescription).

• • •

Some municipalities have taken to providing an opiate antidote, naloxone, to those who request it. The antidote is highly effective if it is administered quickly to someone who is experiencing an opiate overdose.

While I support this measure, it really only scratches the surface of the problem. Providing naloxone to those who are overdosing will save some people from overdosing. But it won't decrease the supply of opiates, and it won't decrease the demand for them, either.

The "war on drugs" didn't decrease the demand for drugs, and it didn't decrease the supply of drugs, either. It just created a much larger prison system. We have way more people imprisoned in 2016 for drug offenses than we did in 1980, and more drug use too.

The supply of drugs isn't going to go away. In the article I read about Canada's fentanyl problem, the authors described the economics of drug distribution. A user can purchase $10,000 worth of raw fentanyl powder, tablet filling supplies, and a tablet press, and sell the end product for as much as $2,000,000 worth of fentanyl tablets.

That is a two-hundred-fold profit. As long as two-hundred-fold profits are available, someone will be willing to sell drugs, regardless of the consequences.

• • •

The drug epidemic is a problem that doesn't have an easy answer. I wish it did. So what follows are not suggested solutions. They are some of my thoughts about the problem:

What if the problem isn't about drugs? The kinds of drugs we are dealing with existed fifty years ago. Some of the drugs are new, but they are really new variations of older drugs. What if the drug epidemic is a symptom of something else?

What if the problem is with us? What if we changed? Suppose the problem is that we seek temporary comfort from permanent problems?

What if the type of pain that we are trying to medicate isn't physical pain? What if the type of pain our society is trying to medicate is spiritual pain? What if opiates can't scratch the kind of itch that we have?

• • •

I don't like to ask these questions. I would much rather stick my head in the sand and hope that the problem goes away.

But no matter how much I stick my fingers in my ears and say "na na na na I can't hear you!" the reality is still there. Right in front of me on a billboard on the Pennsylvania Turnpike.

★ ★ ★ ★ ★
I Need Help

I have a childhood memory of saying "I can do it myself." That strategy worked well when I was two years old and I was learning how to tie my shoelaces. But that strategy doesn't always work now. My life works better when I ask for help, but I still find that the three hardest words to say are "I need help."

• • •

I know some people who need help right now, but they are unable (or unwilling) to ask for it. There is something in our culture (at least there was) that makes asking for help a shameful activity. We have a thread of cultural DNA that says, "I am a pioneer, I am self-made, I don't need help from anyone or anything." Asking for help is seen as a sign of weakness in our culture.

That's nonsense. People with big responsibilities have "ask for help" baked into their job descriptions. CEOs have boards of directors, and presidents and prime ministers have cabinets. Boards of directors and cabinets are there to provide advice and help.

I need help clearing the roads if there is a blizzard. I need help with traffic control if there is a six-car accident ahead of me. I need help with trash pickup, electric and gas service, car repair, income tax preparation, and colonoscopies. I can't do any of those by myself.

It's not only tasks that I need help with. I also need help with decision making. I can make some incredibly bad decisions all by myself. I still have the capacity to think that I know better than everyone else. One example of this is that when I was younger, I decided that I didn't need to change the oil in my car. I ignored the light on the dashboard for several months. (Imagine the expression on the face of the mechanic when he pulled the dipstick out of the engine and there was no oil on the dipstick.) After making a bad decision like that, one of my friends used to ask me, "How is that working for you?" So I've learned to ask for help in my life.

If CEOs and world leaders can ask for help, I should be able to ask for help too. A paradox in my life is that things work much better when I ask for help, but I don't want to. Think about that for a minute. I don't want to do something that works really well for me.

I need help.

★ ★ ★ ★ ★

Off the Record

(I wrote this essay prior to the 2016 presidential election.)

There was a presidential debate last night. One of the remarkable things about the debate, and the campaign, is how much time has been spent defending old emails and old videos. Both candidates recorded things years ago that are now coming back to haunt them.

I am glad that I am not running for office.

• • •

I'm going to say something here, and you may not like it. But I believe it to be true: All of our emails, both personal and professional, are saved. This I know to be true. Most of our telephone communication can be digitized and analyzed electronically. Allow me to explain.

• • •

Last week, Yahoo admitted that they had been scanning the email of all of their users at the request of US intelligence services. I waited for other email providers to denounce this practice. None did. The silence was deafening.

All of our email is stored someplace. Every email that we create, both at work and at home, is stored on a server. If I send you a quick email, and you delete it and I delete it, it is still stored on a server someplace.

The email that you create and receive is stored. If you don't believe me, ask the IT people where you work. Everything is stored and backed up. It can be retrieved later on, for a variety of reasons.

• • •

I used to work at a company where someone wrote a bad email. At the time, I'm sure she didn't think it was so bad. She was having a bad day, and she complained about something to a colleague. But her complaint was written on a day when the company was going through a public-health crisis.

Plaintiffs' attorneys obtained her email during the discovery process, and her email was used in several lawsuits. Many of the lawsuits (class action) resulted in damages of tens of millions of dollars.

I have taken several communications training courses. One of the classic principles in those training courses is to pretend that the email I am about to write is going to appear on the front page of the newspaper tomorrow. Would I still be comfortable sending that email?

• • •

Email isn't the only thing that we are able store and scan. I have a friend who works for a company that digitizes telephone calls. Telephone calls are converted to text, and stored. The text can then be scanned, for a variety of reasons. You consent to this activity every time you call a customer-service center ("your call may be recorded for customer-service training").

Since the technology exists to record telephone calls, digitize them, and then analyze them as text in computers ... do you think it might be possible that this technology is being used for things other than customer-service training?

I'm just saying . . .

· · ·

Much of what we do with our smartphones and our computers is saved, whether we like it or not. The idea that an email is "my email" or a phone call is "my phone call" doesn't exist anymore. I use public networks to send email and phone calls, and as a result, the companies that host those networks have access to my information.

· · ·

I sometimes read articles in newspapers and magazines where the authors use an expression: "off the record." Their sources, in an effort to maintain anonymity, request that certain discussion points not be attributed to a source. In other words, people ask if their conversation can be "off the record." There isn't much left that is off the record.

Just ask Hillary and Donald.

★ ★ ★ ★ ★
Keep Your Eye on the Ball

I write a lot of letters to my family. My book *Can Openers: Essays on Life and Love* is a result of those letters. I wanted to collect all of my letters, and all of my writings, in one place. I used my first book to do that.

I always write a letter to my wife and my daughters at transition times. For my daughters, those transitions included these events:

1. First day of kindergarten, and last day of elementary school
2. First day of middle school, and last day of middle school
3. First day of high school, and graduating high school
4. Passing driver's license test

5. Starting college, and graduating college

My older daughter is starting her first full-time job this week. That is a big transition, so I wrote her a letter. One of the things that most of my transition letters included were some thoughts about "keeping your eye on the ball."

"Keeping your eye on the ball" means a lot of things in our house. In some respects, it means the same as "Who's Your Tribe?" which I discussed at the beginning of this book. In other words ... what is the most important thing in your life? That is a really important question, so I am going to pause, and ask that question again.

What is the most important thing in your life?

• • •

I know a couple of people who have life-threatening diseases. They are fighting for their lives right now. I know that if I ask them what the most important thing is in their lives, they would say "beating this disease."

The other thing I know is that they act consistently with their answer. They have treatments, and appointments, and medication, and therapy—and they show up for all of it.

They know what the most important thing is in their lives, and they act like it.

• • •

When I asked my daughters to "keep your eye on the ball" in my transition letters, I was asking them to focus on what they were doing. I wanted them to obtain a great education, and I thought that if they kept their eyes on the ball (their education), they would obtain a great education. I think I was right.

As my daughters go out into the world, they are going to have to decide what the most important thing is in their lives. That isn't a decision I can make for them, and it isn't a decision I want to make for them, either. I would make the wrong decisions for them, because their hopes and dreams are different than mine.

I don't want them to have the same answer to "What is the most important thing in your life" as I do. What I want is that they know what the most important thing is in their lives, and that they act consistently with that answer.

• • •

I know that you don't want a homework assignment right now, but I am assigning a homework assignment. I want you to answer two questions:

1. What is the most important thing in your life?
2. Are your actions consistent with your answer in number 1?

* * * * *

The Hero's Journey

My wife shared a book with me this week titled *The Invisible Thread* by Laura Schroff and Alex Tresniowski. It's a true story about a young businesswoman who passes a panhandling boy on the streets of New York City. They strike up a lifelong relationship that helps both of them.

They boy endures the most difficult upbringing. He is at times homeless, without food, unsafe, and without any adult direction. Yet he endures, and he does so in the most positive way. He grows up, and becomes a father and a husband, and he has started a small business.

• • •

I signed up for a 105-mile bike marathon a few years ago with two friends. I was not a serious rider. My friends were serious riders, and would often do rides of 50–100 miles.

It was hot, and I was unprepared. I had the wrong type of bike. After 75 miles, I wanted to quit. My friend Pete said, "You can quit, and we will leave you here to die ... or you can finish with us and enjoy the feeling of completing this ride for the rest of your life."

I have no idea where Pete got that from, but we finished, and I will remember the feeling of finishing that ride for the rest of my life.

• • •

I recently read about Angela Duckworth, who won a MacArthur grant (one of the "genius grants") to study grit. She has a new book entitled *Grit*. Her research found that the most common trait among successful Navy SEALs, Ivy League graduates, and spelling bee winners wasn't intelligence, or size, or speed, or income.

It was grit. One definition of grit is "perseverance and passion for long-term goals" (thank you, Wikipedia!).

• • •

Everyone I know who is successful has this quality of perseverance. Every one of them.

Each of them has had to dig deep in themselves and find motivation to keep going, when everything outside of them suggested that they quit. They have all experienced "the hero's journey." They have all gone through hell at some point in their lives, dug deep, and came through their hellish experiences transformed.

• • •

I sometimes forget that other people have had to go through their own personal hells to get where they are today. I wrongly assume that everyone else has an easy, straight path to their successful lives.

I forget that the path to success has a lot of potholes in it, and that successful people have to persevere.

* * * * *

Impatience and Impatiens

I'm impatient. I don't like standing in long lines. I stare at the microwave, wondering why it takes so long to nuke my food.

What I am most impatient about is not knowing.

• • •

Sometimes I make random connections. One of those connections is that "impatience" and "impatiens" sound the same.

I recently planted some impatiens. They make a great addition to a backyard flowerbed. They don't need a lot of care (except for some watering if it doesn't rain for a while), and they are available in a lot of colors.

Planting stuff in the garden is good for me. I get lost in the moment when I am working in the yard. I forget about the outside world. Sometimes the results are really good, and we have color in the backyard all summer long.

Working in my backyard helps me with patience. I know that any work that I do in April is not going to pay dividends immediately. Sometime in September, I will have something colorful to look at.

• • •

I mentioned that I don't like not knowing. For example, if I send meeting invitations, or party invitations, and people don't reply, that bothers me. How am I supposed to run a meeting, or throw a party, if I don't know who is going to attend?

I wrote an essay once called "Sometimes the Answer Is No." That was about dealing with disappointments. But at least when I receive a "no," I know what the answer is.

Not knowing the answer seems worse sometimes.

* * * * *

A House Divided

(This was originally published October 25, 2016 on halwardblog.com.)

(I wrote this prior to a recent election. It is still true ...)

The current political campaign is the most negative one in the history of the US. I'm not taking sides here. Both sides have attacked each other more personally than ever before.

This is true at all levels of elections. I have seen local TV and print ads that claim criminal activities on the part of candidates on both sides of the political spectrum.

When I was younger, political campaigns were like athletic competitions. Everyone wanted to win, of course. But politicians highlighted their own positives. When elections ended, politicians went back to work with each other, trying to serve their constituents.

I miss that.

• • •

Attack ads are sponsored by people who have to work with each other. At the local, state, and federal level, people have to work together to ensure that roads are maintained, bills are paid, and police and fire and emergency services are available.

How does our government return to work on November 9 after this election? How do politicians go back to work, and work with each other? The people who are attacking each other are supposed to show up for work and get work done. How do you work with people who are attacking you, and who you are attacking? How do we recover from this election? How do we put this genie back in the bottle?

• • •

We are fond of chanting "USA" at sporting events and political campaigns. The "U" stands for United. How united are we right now? If we aren't satisfied with the answer, what do we do about that? How do we (can we) get back to a place where we work with each other, instead of against each other?

This election is not an individual transaction that we can walk away from. This isn't a used car negotiation, where we can insult the seller and leave. The seller and the buyer in this transaction are us. The people we are insulting today are people we need to work with on November 9, and beyond.

• • •

Years ago, there was a comic strip called *Pogo*. Pogo once said, "We have met the enemy, and he is us."

How do we stop acting like the enemy is us?

★ ★ ★ ★ ★

The Art of Worrying

A couple of months ago, Theresa received a letter that called her to a jury selection pool. The pool is being selected for a very public murder trial in our state.

People who are selected for this jury will have to travel to north-central Pennsylvania every Sunday night and stay until Friday. They will have to do that every week for what will probably be a three-month trial.

I assumed the worst. I assumed that she would be selected and be gone from home for three months. To make a long story short, she was interviewed in the courtroom for about two minutes, and then she was dismissed.

• • •

A few weeks ago, I started passing blood. "Passing blood" means that my urine was bright red. I'm a healthcare provider, so I remember from my education that urine is supposed to be yellow, not red. Yellow good, red bad.

I had a physician appointment, and then a urologist appointment, then a CAT scan and a cystoscopy. "Cystoscopy" is a fancy word for sticking a TV camera someplace that a TV camera was never designed to go.

And to make a long story short, I'm relieved (really relieved!) to report that I'm clean. The CAT scan and cystoscopy ruled out cancer in my liver, kidneys, bladder, ureters and prostate.

What I'm not so relieved to report is what the urologist said to me at the end of our last appointment. I asked him why I started bleeding, and he said that "it is a normal part of the aging process."

Ouch. I do not want to participate in the aging process. No one asked me if this was a process that I wanted to be a part of.

• • •

I worry a lot. Those of you who know me well know that that is part of my personality. I rarely think about what the best outcome could possibly be. I usually think about the worst possible outcome. One of my friends calls that "catastrophizing."

The good news about worrying is that I sweat a lot of details, both at home and at work. We get a lot of stuff done, because I worry about a lot of stuff. But I spend a lot of time worrying about my wife living 150 miles away for three months, and about me having prostate cancer. Mainly I worry about things that never happen. If worrying was an art, my art would be hanging in museums all around the world.

* * * * *

Don't Be Disruptive

(I wrote this essay in 2017, and published it at halwardblog.com.)

A movie that I want to watch is going to be released in a streaming format next week. I am going to watch it as soon as it is released. I might watch it on my TV. Or maybe on my home computer or a laptop. I might even watch part of it on my telephone.

When I was in high school (back in the Stone Age, in 1976), the VHS tape was invented. That technology was "disruptive," although we didn't call it that at the time. We knew it was revolutionary. People lined up at video-rental stores, like my local West Coast Video store.

In 1995, the DVD was invented. People stopped watching VHS tapes and started watching DVDs.

In 2006, Amazon launched video streaming.

"Renting a video" was a revolutionary concept in 1976. It absolutely revolutionized home entertainment. Now I don't know if there are any video-rental stores still in existence. I am amazed when a disruptive technology is disrupted out of existence.

• • •

Which brings me to cars. I am fascinated by cars. I've written about this before ("Take Me to Work, Siri"). This is a part of our society that is ripe for disruption.

We spend a lot of time and money on cars. I did a search on how much gas America used last year, and the result was 143 billion gallons. At $2.14 a gallon (the 2016 national average), that works out to be about $306 billion per year. Add in $570 billion for new car purchases last year, and our expenditures for cars every year approaches $1 trillion. And that doesn't include maintenance and tolls.

A Department of Transportation report has noted that 1.7 million people drive trucks for a living. That is a lot of salaries and benefits. And many more people drive taxis and limousines.

• • •

One sign of disruption is that Ford Motor Company (a profitable company) recently fired its CEO and announced the layoff of 10% of its global workforce.

Another sign of disruption is that the largest American car company by market capitalization (stock market size) is no longer GM or Ford. It is now Tesla, a company that doesn't make very many cars. At least not yet.

Other signs of disruption include the existence of cars that can park themselves (at least forty of the 2016 and 2017 models can do this) and electric cars (at least fourteen models now available), and there is now testing of self-driving cars. Mapping software that used to require special devices and subscriptions is now included on every smartphone. Cars no longer need to stop at tollbooths.

• • •

Given that there are now fully electric cars, self-parking cars, sophisticated mapping software, and automatic payment at tollbooths, it is only a matter of time until someone puts all of the pieces together.

Someone will figure out how to do it. This isn't just videotapes and home entertainment.

There is a trillion dollars a year riding on this.

* * * * *

Kicking the Can Down the Road

There is an expression in English: "kicking the can down the road." It means not dealing with something. In other words, if I am "kicking the can down the road," I am delaying action on something that I should be acting on right now.

Another word for this is "procrastination." Procrastination was one of the first topics in the book *The Road Less Traveled*, by M. Scott Peck, M.D. He wrote about this topic in a section on discipline.

• • •

We recently decided to do a small remodeling project in our home. Before the work began, we had to clean out and empty two closets. We had used these closets as storage areas for years. Over the last month, we emptied the closets, threw out what we didn't need or want, and sorted the remaining items. There was a lot to go through. We shredded enough paperwork to fill eight green trash bags with shredded paper. When we finished the task of cleaning out those closets, we felt a lot better about completing the task. Why did it take us so many years to do this?

• • •

I have lots of expressions for procrastination. I say,
"I don't want to deal with this right now."
"Can we discuss this later?"
"I am not prepared to have talk about this right now."
And my favorite,
"I don't want to."

• • •

I have learned that I complete some things that I don't want to do, and avoid other things. I have noticed a pattern to those two categories.

I don't want to go to the dentist, or get a colonoscopy, or see the dermatologist, or exercise, or go food shopping, or get an oil change, or schedule a haircut. But for some reason, I do all of those things regularly, on schedule. I add those things to my calendar, I schedule them, and I complete them.

But the things that involve lots of conflict, or emotional stuff ... those are the things that I put off. They seem too messy to me. For whatever reason, I avoid conflict with other people. I just don't like it. So I kick the can down the road on those things that involve conflict.

I know that I am not unique in this. I see other people who are kicking the can down the road about important things in their lives. Really important things. Marriage, relationship, career, health and safety, and money.

• • •

I am going to clean out some more closets in my life.

★ ★ ★ ★ ★
Some Random Thoughts

Bill Lyon of the Philadelphia Inquirer used to write columns with the theme of random thoughts and second thoughts. With apologies to Bill Lyon, this essay is like that—a collage of miscellaneous thoughts.

• • •

Was Vincent van Gogh a successful painter? Of course. He painted over 800 paintings, and drew over 700 sketches and drawings. One painting (a portrait of Dr. Gachet) sold for over $82 million dollars in 1990. Van Gogh paintings are treasured the world over.

But Vincent van Gogh never experienced public recognition as an artist. Supposedly, he only sold one painting in his lifetime. (There are some disputes about this, but he never made a living from his artwork.) He spent much of the last two years of his life in an asylum, where he painted some of his most famous paintings. In 1890, he committed suicide. He died relatively unknown.

• • •

W as Emily Dickinson a successful poet? Of course. She is one of the most acclaimed poets. She wrote almost 1800 poems in her lifetime.

And published only a handful, most of them anonymously.

Emily Dickinson never experienced public recognition as a poet. She died relatively unknown.

• • •

C an you imagine pursuing your dream for your entire life, without any acclaim at all? Can you imagine writing, or painting, or poeting (I just made that word up), without any feedback at all?

• • •

D o young people wear wristwatches anymore? Why not?
Neither of my daughters own a watch.

I understand that smartphones have clocks on them. But still . . .

• • •

T his weekend is "clock change" weekend. Don't forget to change your clocks at 2 a.m. Sunday morning. (Don't forget to change your smoke detector and carbon monoxide detector batteries at the same time.)

How many clocks do you have to change?

I have to change fourteen. You probably do, too, and don't even notice it. We have three cars, three ovens/microwaves, three watches (I have two and Theresa has one), one hanging wall clock, one thermostat, and three alarm clocks. That doesn't count all of the devices that I gave up on changing a long time ago (DVRs, DVD players, etc.)

• • •

How many passwords do you have?
   I have twenty-two user id/password combinations at work, and another thirty-eight at home. Sixty in total, but there really are more than that, I just stopped writing down the ones I don't care about.

One of the ironies of passwords, is that we are often instructed to make them very complicated, so that they can't be hacked. For example, we are supposed to use a combination of upper- and lower-case letters; or letters and numbers, sometimes with, sometimes without special symbols; or non-meaningful letter combinations.

Very good advice.

But now hackers can steal our passwords directly off of a server. It doesn't matter how clever I am with passwords, if a hacker can hack into a server and copy it.

How many letters have you received from companies indicating that their super-secure systems were breached, and that you better change your password anytime in the next ten minutes or so?

Wonderful.

• • •

One last random thought, and this one is a doozy . . .
   How many people die every day?
Seriously.
No one really knows, but here is my answer.

Suppose that there are seven billion people on earth (that number seems accurate, based on the traffic going into work this morning).

Now suppose that the average life expectancy is seventy years.

Seven billion times seventy years equals one hundred million people a year.

One hundred million people a year divided by 365 days in a year, equals 273,972 people dying every day.

That number might be wrong. Maybe there are six billion people on earth, or eight billion. And maybe the life expectancy is sixty years, or eighty years.

The point is ... I'm not exactly sure what the point is, but this is what I think about when I am sitting in traffic on Route 1.

That is why I tell the people in my life that I love them every time I say goodbye. Because I don't know which day is the day I get called up to the big leagues.

Now before you think I am getting grim, I'm not. My plan is to be here for another forty years. Ninety-three years old. And I am willing to discuss contract extensions after that, if there is a need.

But you never know when your time is up. Tell the people you love that you love them.

It can't hurt.

* * * * *

Where Does the Time Go?

(I wrote this after getting together with some high school friends a few years ago ...)

I attended a mini high-school reunion yesterday. I once belonged to a high school fraternity (it's complicated). I had not seen some of these fellows in forty years. I stay in active contact with two of them, and occasional contact with two others. I had not seen the rest in four decades.

These men have had successful lives. There were sixteen people in attendance. Of the sixteen, there were about five attorneys, a physician, two pharmacists, several people who worked in IT, and a couple of fellows who worked in the pharmaceutical industry.

I should note that I've never attended a reunion before. I am not the "reunion type." I am an introvert, and reunions are not introvert territory. I have received invitations for several high school and college reunions, and I've always avoided them before.

Several times, someone asked me, "Do you remember when such and such happened?" The truth is that I did not remember a lot of what was being discussed.

• • •

After the reunion, I decided to visit my old neighborhood. I grew up in Northeast Philadelphia, and lived in the same house for over twenty-five years. I had not been back to that neighborhood since the day of my mothers' funeral, almost nine years ago.

The whole process seemed dreamlike to me. I kept looking for familiar landmarks, but most of them had disappeared. All of the restaurants and most of the shops that I remembered are no longer there.

First I drove past my childhood home.

Then I drove past my elementary school.

Finally I drove past the store where I had my first job.

Things seemed kind of grim to me. I saw four to five homeless men looking for handouts on Roosevelt Boulevard while I was driving.

• • •

On the drive home from the reunion and my old neighborhood, I encountered a detour, and wound up driving right past the hospital where my daughters were born—a place I had not been in sixteen years.

The combination of the reunion, the drive through my old neighborhood, and the drive past the hospital where my daughters were born made for one of the strangest days I've had in years. I came home and closed my eyes for a while. I had to mentally digest everything that had happened. It was fun seeing old classmates. But it was depressing going back to my old neighborhood. And how has sixteen years passed since we brought my younger daughter home?

Where did the time go?!

LETTER CLOSERS

Please allow me sixty seconds for a few thank-yous.

Thank you to my family (Theresa, Heather and Dylan) for all of your support. You are the most loving, patient, and tolerant people I know. May you love anything in life as much as I love each of you.

Thank you to David Wogahn, Erin Willard, and AuthorImprints for turning my lump of coal into a diamond of a book. You let me do what I want to do (write) and you did all of the heavy lifting (editing, formatting, the legal stuff).

Last but not least, thank you to all my faithful readers. I can't name each of you, but in addition to my family, you mean a lot to me. Please keep reading and please keep telling me how I am doing. I pay attention to what you say.

With love,
Hal Ward
September 2019